ENJOYING POETRY
FOUR

A GALAXY
OF POEMS OLD AND NEW

ENJOYING POETRY

A Galaxy

OF POEMS

OLD AND NEW

CHOSEN BY

E. W. PARKER, M.C.

LONGMAN

LONGMAN GROUP LIMITED
London

*Associated companies, branches and representatives
throughout the world*

First published 1962
Seventh impression 1971

ISBN 0 582 34112 4

Decorations by Edward Nolan

*Printed in Hong Kong by
The Hong Kong Printing Press Ltd*

FOREWORD

THE first three books of *Enjoying Poetry* were published in the summer of 1957 under the titles of *Silver and Gold*, *For Delight* and *For Your Pleasure*, and as a result of their success an insistent demand sprang up for a continuation of the Series.

It is this need which Book Four has been planned to meet. Like the other books, it owes part of its contents to my earlier anthologies, but in addition it contains a number of new poems written by contemporary poets in an idiom familiar to young readers.

E. W. P.

ACKNOWLEDGMENTS

WE are indebted to the following for permission to quote copyright material: Mrs. George Bambridge, Messrs. Macmillan & Co. Ltd. and The Macmillan Company of Canada Ltd. for 'Cities and Thrones and Powers' by Rudyard Kipling from *Puck of Pook's Hill*; Mr. Edmund Blunden for 'Almswomen' and 'Forefathers' from *Poems of Many Years*, published by Messrs. William Collins Sons & Co. Ltd.; Mrs. Mary Campbell for 'The Serf' and 'The Zebras' by Roy Campbell; Messrs. Jonathan Cape Ltd. and Henry Holt & Co. Inc., New York, for 'After Apple-Picking', 'The Tuft of Flowers' and 'Stopping by Woods on a Snowy Evening' from *The Collected Poems of Robert Frost*; and Messrs. Jonathan Cape Ltd. for 'The Conflict' and 'The Ecstatic' from *The Collected Poems of C. Day Lewis*; Mr. Charles Causley for 'King's College Chapel' from *Farewell, Aggie Weston*, published by Hand and Flower Press; Messrs. Chatto & Windus Ltd. for 'Strange Meeting' by Wilfred Owen, and 'Evening' by Frederic Prokosch; The Clarendon Press, Oxford, for 'Nightingales' and 'A Passer-by' from *The Shorter Poems of Robert Bridges*; Miss D. E. Collins and Messrs. J. M. Dent & Sons Ltd. for 'In Praise of Dust' by G. K. Chesterton from *The Wild Knight and Other Poems*; The Cresset Press for 'Stormcock in Elder' by Ruth Pitter; Mr. Paul Dehn for 'Fern House at Kew' from *Romantic Landscape*, published by Messrs. Hamish Hamilton, Ltd.; Messrs. J. M. Dent & Sons Ltd. for 'The Swans' by Clifford Dyment, 'Fern Hill' and 'Death Shall Have No Dominion', by Dylan Thomas, from *Collected Poems*; Mr. Patric Dickinson for 'The Kestrel'; Messrs. Gerald Duckworth & Co. Ltd. for 'Cuckoo!' and 'Ha'nacker Mill', by Hilaire Belloc, from *Sonnets and Verse*; Messrs. Faber & Faber Ltd. for 'Caves' by Michael Roberts, 'A Song for Simeon', 'Journey of the Magi' and 'The Hollow Men' by T. S. Eliot, 'Horses' and 'The Combat' by Edwin Muir, 'The Cranes' by Anne Ridler, 'For the Grieg Centenary' by Norman Nicholson, 'He will watch the Hawk', 'I think continually' and 'The Pylons' by Stephen Spender, 'Epilogue',

ACKNOWLEDGMENTS

'Fish in the Unruffled Lakes' and 'Look, Stranger' by W. H. Auden; Mrs. Flecker and Messrs. Martin Secker & Warburg Ltd. for 'The Old Ships' from *Collected Poems* of J. E. Flecker; Mr. Roy Fuller for 'The Giraffes'; Mr. Wilfrid Gibson for 'The Wind and the Rain' from *The Golden Room*; Mr. Robert Graves for '1805' from *Collected Poems 1959*, published by Messrs. Cassell & Co. Ltd.; Harcourt, Brace & Co. Inc., New York, for 'Portrait of a Machine' by Louis Untermeyer from *Roast Leviathan*, copyright 1923 Harcourt Brace, renewed 1951 by Louis Untermeyer; The Trustees of the Hardy Estate and Messrs. Macmillan & Co. Ltd. for 'In the "Time of the Breaking of Nations"', 'In the British Museum' and 'On a Midsummer Eve' from *Collected Poems of Thomas Hardy*; Messrs. Rupert Hart-Davis Ltd. for 'Wiltshire Downs' by Andrew Young; Messrs. William Heinemann Ltd. for 'Giraffes' and 'Nothing Grows Old' by Phœbe Hesketh from *No Time for Cowards*; Mr. Ralph Hodgson and Messrs. Macmillan & Co. Ltd. for 'The Song of Honour' from *Poems*; The Society of Authors as the literary representatives of the Trustees of the Estate of the late A. E. Housman for 'Bredon Hill', 'Loveliest of Trees' and 'When summer's end is nighing' from *Collected Poems*, published by Messrs. Jonathan Cape Ltd.; The Estate of the late Mrs. Frieda Lawrence for 'Bat' and 'Piano' from *The Collected Poems of D. H. Lawrence*; The Macmillan Company of Canada Ltd. for 'For Dinah, the Adeneys' Cat' from *The Hangman Ties the Holly* by Anne Wilkinson; The Literary Trustees of Walter de la Mare and The Society of Authors as their representatives for 'An Epitaph', 'Evening', 'Fare Well', 'Music' and 'The Scribe'; Messrs. John Murray (Publishers) Ltd. for 'Norfolk' and 'Seaside Golf' by John Betjeman from *Collected Poems*; The Oxford University Press for 'Pied Beauty' and 'As Kingfishers catch fire' by Gerard Manley Hopkins; the late Eden Phillpotts for 'Written on Dew'; the representative of Mr. Ezra Pound for 'The Eyes'; Miss Kathleen Raine for 'Seen in a Glass' from *Collected Poems*, published by Messrs. Hamish Hamilton Ltd.; Messrs. Routledge & Kegan Paul Ltd. for 'Greenwich Observatory' and 'Wordsworth' by Sidney Keyes from *Collected Poems*; The Hon. Victoria Sackville-West for 'Making Cider'; The Hon. Lady Salmond for 'Into Battle' by Julian Grenfell; Mr. Siegfried Sassoon for 'Everyone Sang' from *War Poems*; Miss E. J. Scovell and The Cresset Press for 'A Dark World'; Messrs. Sidgwick & Jackson Ltd. and Messrs. McClelland & Stewart Ltd., Toronto, for 'Clouds', 'Peace' and 'The Soldier' from *The Collected Poems of Rupert Brooke*; Mr. Osbert Sitwell for 'On the Coast of Coromandel' from *Selected Poems*, published by Messrs. Gerald Duckworth & Co. Ltd.; The Society of Authors, Dr. John Masefield, O.M., and The Macmillan Company, New York, for 'Beauty' and 'On Malvern Hill'; Mrs. Helen Thomas for 'Words' and 'If I should ever by Chance' by Edward Thomas; Mr. R. S. Thomas for 'The Lonely Farmer' from *Song at the Year's Turning*, published by Messrs. Rupert Hart-Davis Ltd.; Mrs. W. B. Yeats and Messrs. Macmillan & Co. Ltd. for 'Sailing to Byzantium', 'Aedh wishes for the Cloths of Heaven', 'An Irish Airman foresees his Death', 'The Wild Swans at Coole', 'When you are old' from *Collected Poems of W. B. Yeats*; and Christopher Middleton for 'Flight Into Egypt' from *Torse 3*, (Longmans, 1962).

———

I wish to thank my old friend Professor Gurrey for his kindness in looking at the selection at an early stage and for his valuable suggestions.

E. W. P.

CONTENTS

PART ONE

ix

CONTENTS

CONTENTS

CONTENTS

CONTENTS

CONTENTS

PART TWO

CONTENTS

CONTENTS

CONTENTS

CONTENTS

ENJOYING POETRY
FOUR

A GALAXY
OF POEMS OLD AND NEW

Edward

'Why does your brand sae drop wi' blude,
  Edward, Edward?
Why does your brand sae drop wi' blude,
  And why sae sad gang ye, O?'—
'O I hae kill'd my hawk sae gude,
  Mither, Mither;
O I hae kill'd my hawk sae gude,
  And I had nae mair but he, O.'

'Your hawk's blude was never sae red,
  Edward, Edward;
Your hawk's blude was never sae red,
  My dear son, I tell thee, O.'—
'O I hae kill'd my red-roan steed,
  Mither, Mither;
O I hae kill'd my red-roan steed,
  That erst was sae fair and free, O.'

'Your steed was auld, and ye hae got mair,
  Edward, Edward;
Your steed was auld, and ye hae got mair;
  Some other dule ye dree, O.'—
'O I hae kill'd my father dear,
  Mither, Mither;
O I hae kill'd my father dear,
  Alas, and wae is me, O!'

'And whatten penance will ye dree for that,
   Edward, Edward?
Whatten penance will ye dree for that?
   My dear son, now tell me, O.'—
'I'll set my feet in yonder boat,
   Mither, Mither;
I'll set my feet in yonder boat,
   And I'll fare over the sea, O.'

'And what will ye do wi' your tow'rs and your ha',
   Edward, Edward?
And what will ye do wi' your tow'rs and your ha',
   That were sae fair to see, O?'—
'I'll let them stand till they doun fa',
   Mither, Mither;
I'll let them stand till they doun fa',
   For here never mair maun I be, O.'

'And what will ye leave to your bairns and your wife,
   Edward, Edward?
And what will ye leave to your bairns and your wife,
   When ye gang owre the sea, O?'—
'The warld's room: let them beg through life,
   Mither, Mither;
The warld's room: let them beg through life:
   For them never mair will I see, O.'

'And what will ye leave to your ain mither dear,
   Edward, Edward?
And what will ye leave to your ain mither dear,
   My dear son, now tell me, O?'—

'The curse of hell frae me sall ye bear,
　Mither, Mither;
The curse of hell frae me sall ye bear:
　Sic counsels ye gave to me, O!'
ANONYMOUS

Helen of Kirconnell

I wish I were where Helen lies,
Night and day on me she cries;
O that I were where Helen lies,
　On fair Kirconnell lea!

Curst be the heart that thought the thought,
And curst the hand that fired the shot,
When in my arms burd Helen dropt,
　And died to succour me!

O think na ye my heart was sair,
When my Love dropt and spak nae mair?
There did she swoon wi' meikle care,
　On fair Kirconnell lea.

As I went down the waterside,
None but my foe to be my guide,
None but my foe to be my guide,
　On fair Kirconnell lea;

I lighted down, my sword to draw,
I hackèd him in pieces sma',
I hackèd him in pieces sma',
  For her sake that died for me.

O Helen fair, beyond compare!
I'll mak a garland o' thy hair,
Shall bind my heart for evermair,
  Until the day I dee!

O that I were where Helen lies!
Night and day on me she cries;
Out of my bed she bids me rise,
  Says, 'Haste, and come to me!'

O Helen fair! O Helen chaste!
If I were with thee, I'd be blest,
Where thou lies low and taks thy rest,
  On fair Kirconnell lea.

I wish my grave were growing green,
A winding-sheet drawn owre my een,
And I in Helen's arms lying,
  On fair Kirconnel lea.

I wish I were where Helen lies!
Night and day on me she cries:
And I am weary of the skies,
  For her sake that died for me.

ANONYMOUS

4

Vox Ultima Crucis

Tarye no lenger; toward thyn herytage
Hast on thy weye, and be of ryght good chere.
Go eche day onward on thy pylgrymage;
Thynke howe short tyme thou shalt abyden here.
Thy place is bygged above the sterres clere,
Noon erthly palys wrought in so statly wyse.
Come on, my frend, my brother most entere!
For the I offered my blood in sacryfice.

bygged = built.   *palys* = palace.

JOHN LYDGATE

The Appeal

An Earnest Suit to his Unkind Mistress not to Forsake him

And wilt thou leave me thus?
  Say nay, say nay, for shame,
  —To save thee from the blame
  Of all my grief and grame;
And wilt thou leave me thus?
  Say nay, say nay!

And wilt thou leave me thus,
  That hath loved thee so long
  In wealth and woe among?
  And is thy heart so strong
As for to leave me thus?
  Say nay, say nay!

And wilt thou leave me thus,
　That hath given thee my heart
　Never for to depart
　Neither for pain nor smart:
And wilt thou leave me thus?
　Say nay, say nay!

And wilt thou leave me thus,
　And have no more pitye
　Of him that loveth thee?
　Helas! thy cruelty!
And wilt thou leave me thus?
　Say nay! say nay!

SIR THOMAS WYATT

grame = sorrow.　　　*among* = all the time.
　　Helas = other versions give ' Alas.'

Coming Homeward out of Spain

O raging seas, and mighty Neptune's reign!
　In monstrous hills that throwest thyself so high,
That with thy floods dost beat the shores of Spain,
　And break the cliffs that dare thy force envy.

Cease now thy rage, and lay thine ire aside,
　And thou that hast the governance of all,
O mighty God grant weather, wind, and tide,
　Till on my country coast our anchor fall.

BARNABE GOOGE

There is a Lady Sweet and Kind

There is a Lady sweet and kind,
Was never face so pleased my mind;
I did but see her passing by,
And yet I love her till I die.

Her gesture, motion, and her smiles,
Her wit, her voice, my heart beguiles,
Beguiles my heart, I know not why,
And yet I love her till I die.

Cupid is wingèd and doth range,
Her country so my love doth change:
But change the earth, or change the sky,
Yet will I love her till I die.

ANONYMOUS

Love not me for Comely Grace

Love not me for comely grace,
For my pleasing eye or face,
Nor for any outward part,
No, nor for my constant heart:
  For these may fail or turn to ill,
    So thou and I shall sever:
Keep, therefore, a true woman's eye,
And love me still, but know not why—
    So hast thou the same reason still
      To doat upon me ever!

ANONYMOUS

Weep you no more, Sad Fountains

Weep you no more, sad fountains;
  What need you flow so fast?
Look how the snowy mountains
  Heaven's sun doth gently waste.
    But my sun's heavenly eyes
      View not your weeping,
      That now lies sleeping
    Softly, now softly lies
      Sleeping.

Sleep is a reconciling,
  A rest that peace begets.
Doth not the sun rise smiling
  When fair at even he sets?
    Rest you then, rest, sad eyes,
      Melt not in weeping,
      While she lies sleeping
    Softly, now softly lies
      Sleeping.

ANONYMOUS

Sister, Awake!

Sister, awake! close not your eyes!
  The day her light discloses,
And the bright morning doth arise
  Out of her bed of roses.

See the clear sun, the world's bright eye,
  In at our window peeping;
Lo, how he blusheth to espy
  Us idle wenches sleeping!

Therefore awake! make haste, I say,
  And let us, without staying,
All in our gowns of green so gay,
  Into the Park a-maying!

ANONYMOUS

The Passionate Man's Pilgrimage

Give me my scallop-shell of quiet,
My staff of faith to walk upon,
My scrip of joy, immortal diet,
My bottle of salvation,
My gown of glory, hope's true gage,
And thus I'll take my pilgrimage.

Blood must be my body's balmer,
No other balm will there be given,

Whilst my soul like a white palmer
Travels to the land of heaven,
Over the silver mountains,
Where spring the nectar fountains;
And there I'll kiss
The bowl of bliss,
And drink my everlasting fill
On every milken hill.
My soul will be a-dry before,
But after it will thirst no more.

And by the happy blissful way
More peaceful pilgrims I shall see,
That have shook off their gowns of clay
And go apparelled fresh like me.
I'll bring them first
To slake their thirst,
And then to taste those nectar suckets,
At the clear wells
Where sweetness dwells,
Drawn up by saints in crystal buckets.

And when our bottles and all we
Are filled with immortality,
Then the holy paths we'll travel,
Strewed with rubies thick as gravel,
Ceilings of diamonds, sapphire floors,
High walls of coral and pearl bowers.

From thence to heaven's bribeless hall
Where no corrupted voices brawl,
No conscience molten into gold,
Nor forged accusers bought and sold,

No cause deferred, nor vain-spent journey,
For there Christ is the King's Attorney,
Who pleads for all without degrees,
And he hath angels, but no fees.

When the grand twelve million jury
Of our sins and direful fury
'Gainst our souls black verdicts give,
Christ pleads his death, and then we live.
Be thou my speaker, taintless pleader,
Unblotted lawyer, true proceeder;
Thou movest salvation even for alms,
Not with a bribèd lawyer's palms.

And this is my eternal plea
To him that made heaven, earth, and sea:
Seeing my flesh must die so soon,
And want a head to dine next noon,
Just at the stroke when my veins start and spread,
Set on my soul an everlasting head.
Then am I ready, like a palmer fit,
To tread those blest paths which before I writ.

Lines written during his imprisonment in the Tower of London

SIR WALTER RALEIGH

Epitaph

Even such is Time, which takes in trust
Our youth, our joys, and all we have,
And pays us but with age and dust ;
Who in the dark and silent grave,
When we have wandered all our ways,
Shuts up the story of our days :
And from which earth, and grave, and dust,
The Lord shall raise me up, I trust.

*Lines found in his Bible in the Gatehouse at Westminster on the
night before his execution*

SIR WALTER RALEIGH

Walsinghame

'As you came from the holy land
    Of Walsinghame,
Met you not with my true love
    By the way as you came ?'

'How shall I know your true love,
    That have met many one
As I went to the holy land,
    That have come, that have gone ?'

'She is neither white nor brown,
   But as the heavens fair,
There is none hath a form so divine
   In the earth or the air.'

'Such an one did I meet, good Sir,
   Such an angelic face,
Who like a queen, like a nymph did appear
   By her gait, by her grace.'

'She hath left me here all alone,
   All alone as unknown,
Who sometimes did me lead with herself,
   And me loved as her own.'

'What's the cause that she leaves you alone
   And a new way doth take,
Who loved you once as her own
   And her joy did you make?'

'I have loved her all my youth,
   But now old as you see,
Love likes not the falling fruit
   From the withered tree.'

'Know that Love is a careless child,
   And forgets promise past;
He is blind, he is deaf when he list
   And in faith never fast.'

'His desire is a dureless content
   And a trustless joy;

He is won with a world of despair
 And is lost with a toy.'

'Of womenkind such indeed is the love
 Or the word love abused,
Under which many childish desires
 And conceits are excused.'

'But love is a durable fire
 In the mind ever burning;
Never sick, never old, never dead,
 From itself never turning.'

      SIR WALTER RALEIGH

Like as a Ship that through the Ocean wide

Like as a ship that through the ocean wide
 By conduct of some star doth make her way,
Whenas a storm hath dimmed her trusty guide,
 Out of her course doth wander far astray:

So I whose star, that wont with her bright ray
Me to direct, with clouds is overcast,
   Do wander now in darkness and dismay,
Through hidden perils round about me placed.
Yet hope I well, that when this storm is past,
   My Helice, the lodestar of my life,
Will shine again, and look on me at last,
   With lovely light to clear my cloudy grief.
Till then I wander, care-full, comfortless,
In secret sorrow and sad pensiveness.

EDMUND SPENSER

One Day as I unwarily did gaze

One day as I unwarily did gaze
   On those fair eyes my love's immortal light;
The whiles my 'stonished heart stood in amaze,
   Through sweet illusion of her looks' delight.
   I mote perceive how in her glancing sight,
Legions of loves with little wings did fly:
   Darting their deadly arrows fiery bright,
At every rash beholder passing by.
One of those archers closely I did spy,
   Aiming his arrow at my very heart:
When suddenly with twinkle of her eye,
   The damsel broke his misintended dart.
Had she not so done, sure I had been slain,
Yet as it was, I hardly 'scaped with pain.

EDMUND SPENSER

*My True Love hath my Heart**

My true love hath my heart and I have his,
    By just exchange one for another given;
I hold his dear, and mine he cannot miss,
    There never was a better bargain driven.
        My true love hath my heart and I have his.

His heart in me keeps him and me in one,
    My heart in him his thoughts and senses guides;
He loves my heart, for once it was his own:
    I cherish his, because in me it bides.
        My true love hath my heart and I have his.

SIR PHILIP SIDNEY

* There is another version in *Arcadia*.

With how Sad Steps, O Moon

With how sad steps, O Moon, thou climb'st the skies!
    How silently, and with how wan a face!
    What! may it be that even in heavenly place
That busy archer his sharp arrows tries?
Sure, if that long-with-love-acquainted eyes
    Can judge of love, thou feel'st a lover's case;
    I read it in thy looks; thy languished grace
To me, that feel the like, thy state descries.

16

Then, even of fellowship, O Moon, tell me,
  Is constant love deemed there but want of wit?
Are beauties there as proud as here they be?
  Do they above love to be loved, and yet
    Those lovers scorn whom that love doth possess?
    Do they call virtue there ungratefulness?

SIR PHILIP SIDNEY

A Farewell to Arms

To Queen Elizabeth

His golden locks Time hath to silver turned;
  O Time too swift, O swiftness never ceasing!
His youth 'gainst time and age hath ever spurned,
  But spurned in vain; youth waneth by increasing:
Beauty, strength, youth, are flowers but fading seen;
Duty, faith, love, are roots, and ever green.

His helmet now shall make a hive for bees;
  And, lovers' sonnets turned to holy psalms,
A man-at-arms must now serve on his knees,
  And feed on prayers, which are age's alms:
But though from court to cottage he depart,
His Saint is sure of his unspotted heart.

And when he saddest sits in homely cell,
  He'll teach his swains this carol for a song:
'Blest be the hearts that wish my sovereign well,
  Curst be the souls that think her any wrong!'
Goddess, allow this agèd man his right,
To be your beadsman now, that was your knight.

GEORGE PEELE

The Description of Sir Geoffrey Chaucer

His stature was not very tall,
Lean he was, his legs were small,
Hos'd within a stock of red,
A buttoned bonnet on his head,
From under which did hang, I ween,
Silver hairs both bright and sheen.
His beard was white, trimmèd round,
His countenance blithe and merry found.
A sleeveless jacket large and wide,
With many plaits and skirtès side,
Of water camlet did he wear;
A whittle by his belt he bare,
His shoes were cornèd, broad before,
His inkhorn at his side he wore,
And in his hand he bore a book.
Thus did this ancient poet look.

ROBERT GREENE

side = long.   *whittle* = knife.   *cornèd* = pointed.

The Parting

Since there's no help, come let us kiss and part.
Nay, I have done; you get no more of me,
And I am glad, yea, glad with all my heart,
That thus so cleanly I myself can free;
Shake hands for ever, cancel all our vows,
And when we meet at any time again,

Be it not seen in either of our brows
That we one jot of former love retain.
Now at the last gasp of Love's latest breath,
When, his pulse failing, Passion speechless lies,
When Faith is kneeling by his bed of death,
And Innocence is closing up his eyes,
   Now if thou wouldst, when all have given him over,
   From death to life thou mightst him yet recover.

MICHAEL DRAYTON

The Passionate Shepherd to his Love

Come live with me and be my Love,
And we will all the pleasures prove
That hills and valleys, dale and field,
And all the craggy mountains yield.

There will we sit upon the rocks
And see the shepherds feed their flocks,
By shallow rivers, to whose falls
Melodious birds sing madrigals.

There will I make thee beds of roses
And a thousand fragrant posies,
A cap of flowers, and a kirtle
Embroider'd all with leaves of myrtle.

A gown made of the finest wool,
Which from our pretty lambs we pull,
Fair linèd slippers for the cold,
With buckles of the purest gold.

A belt of straw and ivy buds
With coral clasps and amber studs :
And if these pleasures may thee move,
Come live with me and be my Love.

Thy silver dishes for thy meat
As precious as the gods do eat,
Shall on an ivory table be
Prepared each day for thee and me.

The shepherd swains shall dance and sing
For thy delight each May-morning :
If these delights thy mind may move,
Then live with me and be my Love.

CHRISTOPHER MARLOWE

Sonnet xii

When I do count the clock that tells the time,
And see the brave day sunk in hideous night;
When I behold the violet past prime,
And sable curls all silvered o'er with white;
When lofty trees I see barren of leaves,
Which erst from heat did canopy the herd,
And summer's green all girded up in sheaves,

Borne on the bier with white and bristly beard;
Then of thy beauty do I question make,
That thou among the wastes of time must go,
Since sweets and beauties do themselves forsake
And die as fast as they see others grow;
    And nothing 'gainst Time's scythe can make defence
    Save breed, to brave him when he takes thee hence.

WILLIAM SHAKESPEARE

Sonnet xviii

Shall I compare thee to a summer's day?
Thou art more lovely and more temperate:
Rough winds do shake the darling buds of May,
And summer's lease hath all too short a date:
Sometime too hot the eye of heaven shines,
And often is his gold complexion dimmed;
And every fair from fair sometime declines,
By chance, or nature's changing course untrimmed;
But thy eternal summer shall not fade,
Nor lose possession of that fair thou ow'st,
Nor shall death brag thou wander'st in his shade,
When in eternal lines to time thou grow'st;
    So long as men can breathe, or eyes can see,
    So long lives this, and this gives life to thee.

WILLIAM SHAKESPEARE

Sonnet xxix

When in disgrace with fortune and men's eyes
I all alone beweep my outcast state,
And trouble deaf heaven with my bootless cries,
And look upon myself, and curse my fate,
Wishing me like to one more rich in hope,
Featured like him, like him with friends possessed,
Desiring this man's art, and that man's scope,
With what I most enjoy contented least;
Yet in these thoughts myself almost despising—
Haply I think on thee, and then my state,
Like to the lark at break of day arising
From sullen earth, sings hymns at heaven's gate;
    For thy sweet love rememb'red such wealth brings
    That then I scorn to change my state with kings.

WILLIAM SHAKESPEARE

Sonnet xxx

When to the sessions of sweet silent thought
I summon up remembrance of things past,
I sigh the lack of many a thing I sought,
And with old woes new wail my dear time's waste:
Then can I drown an eye, unused to flow,
For precious friends hid in death's dateless night,
And weep afresh love's long-since-cancell'd woe,
And moan the expense of many a vanish'd sight:
Then can I grieve at grievances foregone,

And heavily from woe to woe tell o'er
The sad account of fore-bemoanèd moan,
Which I new pay as if not paid before.
    But if the while I think on thee, dear friend,
    All losses are restored and sorrows end.

WILLIAM SHAKESPEARE

Sonnet lxv

Since brass, nor stone, nor earth, nor boundless sea,
But sad mortality o'er-sways their power,
How with this rage shall beauty hold a plea,
Whose action is no stronger than a flower?
O, how shall summer's honey breath hold out
Against the wreckful siege of battering days,
When rocks impregnable are not so stout,
Nor gates of steel so strong, but Time decays?
O fearful meditation! where, alack,
Shall Time's best jewel from Time's chest lie hid?
Or what strong hand can hold his swift foot back?
Or who his spoil of beauty can forbid?
    O, none, unless this miracle have might,
    That in black ink my love may still shine bright.

WILLIAM SHAKESPEARE

Sonnet lxxiii

That time of year thou may'st in me behold
When yellow leaves, or none, or few, do hang
Upon those boughs which shake against the cold,
Bare ruined choirs, where late the sweet birds sang.
In me thou see'st the twilight of such day
As after sunset fadeth in the west;
Which by and by black night doth take away,
Death's second self, that seals up all in rest.
In me thou see'st the glowing of such fire,
That on the ashes of his youth doth lie,
As on the death-bed whereon it must expire,
Consumed with that which it was nourished by.
  This thou perceivest, which makes thy love more strong,
  To love that well which thou must leave ere long.

WILLIAM SHAKESPEARE

Sonnet cvi

When in the chronicle of wasted time
I see descriptions of the fairest wights,
And beauty making beautiful old rime,
In praise of ladies dead and lovely knights,

Then, in the blazon of sweet beauty's best,
Of hand, of foot, of lip, of eye, of brow,
I see their antique pen would have express'd
Even such a beauty as you master now.
So all their praises are but prophecies
Of this our time, all you prefiguring;
And, for they look'd but with divining eyes,
They had nòt skill enough your worth to sing:
　For we, which now behold these present days,
　Have eyes to wonder, but lack tongues to praise.

WILLIAM SHAKESPEARE

Sonnet cxvi

Let me not to the marriage of true minds
Admit impediments.　Love is not love
Which alters when it alteration finds,
Or bends with the remover to remove:
O no, it is an ever-fixèd mark,
That looks on tempests and is never shaken;
It is the star to every wandering bark,
Whose worth's unknown, although his height be taken.
Love's not Time's fool, though rosy lips and cheeks
Within his bending sickle's compass come;
Love alters not with his brief hours and weeks,
But bears it out even to the edge of doom.
　If this be error, and upon me proved,
　I never writ, nor no man ever loved.

WILLIAM SHAKESPEARE

O Mistress Mine

FROM *TWELFTH NIGHT*

O mistress mine, where are you roaming?
O! stay and hear; your true love's coming,
   That can sing both high and low.
Trip no further, pretty sweeting;
Journeys end in lovers meeting,
   Every wise man's son doth know.

What is love? 'tis not hereafter;
Present mirth hath present laughter;
   What's to come is still unsure:
In delay there lies no plenty;
Then come kiss me, sweet and twenty,
   Youth's a stuff will not endure.

WILLIAM SHAKESPEARE

Fear no more the Heat o' the Sun

FROM *CYMBELINE*

Fear no more the heat o' the sun,
   Nor the furious winter's rages;
Thou thy worldly task hast done,
   Home art gone, and ta'en thy wages;
Golden lads and girls all must,
As chimney-sweepers, come to dust.

Fear no more the frown o' the great,
   Thou art past the tyrant's stroke;
Care no more to clothe and eat;
   To thee the reed is as the oak;
The sceptre, learning, physic, must
All follow this, and come to dust.

Fear no more the lightning-flash,
   Nor the all-dreaded thunder-stone;
Fear not slander, censure rash;
   Thou hast finish'd joy and moan:
All lovers young, all lovers must
Consign to thee, and come to dust.

No exorciser harm thee!
Nor no witchcraft charm thee!
Ghost unlaid forbear thee!
Nothing ill come near thee!
Quiet consummation have;
And renownèd be thy grave!

WILLIAM SHAKESPEARE

Song to Imogen

FROM *CYMBELINE*

Hark! hark! the lark at heaven's gate sings,
   And Phoebus 'gins arise,
His steeds to water at those springs
   On chalic'd flowers that lies;
And winking Mary-buds begin
   To ope their golden eyes:
With every thing that pretty is,
   My lady sweet, arise!
     Arise, arise!

WILLIAM SHAKESPEARE

Come away, come away, Death

FROM *TWELFTH NIGHT*

Come away, come away, death,
   And in sad cypress let me be laid.
Fly away, fly away, breath;
   I am slain by a fair cruel maid.
My shroud of white, stuck all with yew,
     O! prepare it.
My part of death, no one so true
     Did share it.

Not a flower, not a flower sweet,
   On my black coffin let there be strown;
Not a friend, not a friend greet

My poor corse, where my bones shall be thrown.
A thousand thousand sighs to save,
    Lay me, O! where
Sad true lover never find my grave,
    To weep there.

WILLIAM SHAKESPEARE

Take, O Take

FROM *MEASURE FOR MEASURE*

Take, O take those lips away,
    That so sweetly were forsworn,
And those eyes, the break of day,
    Lights that do mislead the morn;
But my kisses bring again,
                bring again,
Seals of love, but sealed in vain,
                sealed in vain.

WILLIAM SHAKESPEARE

A Casket Song

FROM *THE MERCHANT OF VENICE*

Tell me where is fancy bred,
    Or in the heart or in the head?
How begot, how nourished?
    Reply, reply.

It is engender'd in the eyes,
    With gazing fed; and fancy dies
In the cradle where it lies.
    Let us all ring fancy's knell:
    I'll begin it,—Ding, dong, bell.
All. Ding, dong, bell.

WILLIAM SHAKESPEARE

Full Fathom Five thy Father lies

FROM *THE TEMPEST*

Full fathom five thy father lies;
    Of his bones are coral made;
Those are pearls that were his eyes:
    Nothing of him that doth fade,
But doth suffer a sea-change
Into something rich and strange:
Sea nymphs hourly ring his knell.
                    Ding-dong!
Hark! now I hear them,
                    Ding-dong, bell!

WILLIAM SHAKESPEARE

Who is Silvia?

FROM *TWO GENTLEMEN OF VERONA*

Who is Silvia? what is she,
   That all our swains commend her?
Holy, fair, and wise is she;
   The heaven such grace did lend her,
That she might admirèd be.

Is she kind as she is fair?
   For beauty lives with kindness:
Love doth to her eyes repair,
   To help him of his blindness;
And, being helped, inhabits there.

Then to Silvia let us sing,
   That Silvia is excelling;
She excels each mortal thing
   Upon the dull earth dwelling;
To her let us garlands bring.

WILLIAM SHAKESPEARE

Ophelia's Song

FROM *HAMLET*

How should I your true love know
   From another one?
By his cockle hat and staff,
   And his sandal shoon.

He is dead and gone, lady,
   He is dead and gone;
At his head a grass-green turf,
   At his heels a stone.

White his shroud as the mountain snow,
   Larded with sweet flowers;
Which bewept to the grave did go
   With true-love showers.

WILLIAM SHAKESPEARE

There is a Garden in her Face

There is a garden in her face,
   Where roses and white lilies grow;
A heavenly paradise is that place,
   Wherein all pleasant fruits do grow.
There cherries grow which none may buy,
Till 'Cherry-ripe' themselves do cry.

Those cherries fairly do enclose
   Of orient pearl a double row,
Which when her lovely laughter shows,
   They look like rose-buds fill'd with snow.
Yet them nor peer nor prince can buy,
Till 'Cherry-ripe' themselves do cry.

Her eyes like angels watch them still;
   Her brows like bended bows do stand,
Threatening with piercing frowns to kill
   All that attempt with eye or hand
Those sacred cherries to come nigh,
Till 'Cherry-ripe' themselves do cry.

THOMAS CAMPION

The Bounty of our Age

To see a strange outlandish fowl,
A quaint baboon, an ape, an owl,
A dancing bear, a giant's lone,
A foolish engine move alone,

33

A morris dance, a puppet-play,
Mad Tom to sing a roundelay,
A woman dancing on a rope,
Bull-baiting also at the *Hope*,
A rhymer's jests, a juggler's cheats,
A tumbler showing cunning feats,
Or players acting on the stage,—
There goes the bounty of our age;
   But unto any pious motion
   There's little coin and less devotion.

HENRY FARLEY

On his Mistress, the Queen of Bohemia

You meaner Beauties of the Night,
That poorly satisfie our Eyes
More by your number, than your light,
You Common people of the Skies;
   What are you when the Sun shall rise?

You curious Chanters of the wood,
That warble forth Dame Nature's layes,
Thinking your Voices understood
By your weak accents; what's your praise
   When Philomel her voice shall raise?

You Violets, that first appear,
By your pure purple mantles known,
Like the proud Virgins of the year,
As if the Spring were all your own;
   What are you when the Rose is blown?

So, when my Mistress shall be seen
In Form and Beauty of her mind,
By Vertue first, then Choice a Queen,
Tell me, if she were not designed
   Th' Eclipse and Glory of her kind?

SIR HENRY WOTTON

The Basket-maker's Song

FROM *PATIENT GRISSELL*

Art thou poor, yet hast thou golden slumbers?
   O sweet content!
Art thou rich, yet is thy mind perplex'd?
   O punishment!
Dost thou laugh to see how fools are vex'd
To add to golden numbers, golden numbers?
O sweet content! O sweet content!
   Work apace, apace, apace, apace;
   Honest labour bears a lovely face;
Then hey nonny nonny, hey nonny nonny!

THOMAS DEKKER

Canst drink the waters of the crispèd spring?
  O sweet content!
Swim'st thou in wealth, yet sink'st in thine own tears?
  O punishment!
Then he that patiently want's burden bears,
No burden bears, but is a king, a king!
O sweet content! O sweet content!
  Work apace, apace, apace, apace;
  Honest labour bears a lovely face;
Then hey nonny nonny, hey nonny nonny!

THOMAS DEKKER

Death, be not Proud

Death be not proud, though some have called thee
Mighty and dreadful, for thou art not so,
For those whom thou think'st thou dost overthrow,
Die not, poor death, nor yet canst thou kill me.
From rest and sleep, which but thy pictures be,
Much pleasure then from thee, much more must flow,
And soonest our best men with thee do go,
Rest of their bones, and souls' delivery.
Thou'rt slave to Fate, Chance, kings, and desperate men,
And dost with poison, war, and sickness dwell,
And poppy or charms can make us sleep as well,
And better than thy stroke; why swell'st thou then?
One short sleep past, we wake eternally,
And death shall be no more: death, thou shalt die.

JOHN DONNE

A Hymn to God the Father

Wilt thou forgive that sin where I begun,
   Which was my sin, though it were done before?
Wilt thou forgive that sin through which I run
   And do run still, though still I do deplore?
     When thou hast done, thou hast not done,
      For I have more.

Wilt thou forgive that sin, by which I have won
   Others to sin, and made my sin their door?
Wilt thou forgive that sin which I did shun
   A year or two, but wallowed in a score?
     When thou hast done, thou hast not done,
      For I have more.

I have a sin of fear that when I have spun
   My last thread, I shall perish on the shore;
Swear by thy self that at my Death, thy Son
   Shall shine as he shines now, and heretofore;
     And having done that, thou hast done,
      I fear no more.

JOHN DONNE

At the Round Earth's Imagin'd Corners

At the round earth's imagin'd corners blow
Your trumpets, Angels, and arise, arise
From death, you numberlesse infinities
Of soules, and to your scattered bodies goe,
All whom the flood did, and fires shall o'erthrow,
All whom warre, dearth, age, agues, tyrannies,
Despaire, law, chance, hath slaine, and you whose eyes
Shall behold God, and never tast death's woe.
But let them sleepe, Lord, and mee mourne a space,
For, if above all these, my sinnes abound,
'Tis late to aske abundance of thy grace,
When wee are there; here on this lowly ground,
Teach mee how to repent, for that's as good
As if thou hadst seal'd my pardon with Thy blood.

JOHN DONNE

To Celia

FROM *THE FOREST*

Drink to me only with thine eyes,
    And I will pledge with mine;
Or leave a kiss but in the cup
    And I'll not look for wine.
The thirst that from the soul doth rise
    Doth ask a drink divine:
But might I of Jove's *Nectar* sup,
    I would not change for thine.

I sent thee, late, a rosy wreath,
  Not so much honouring thee
As giving it a hope, that there
  It could not withered be.
But thou thereon didst only breathe,
  And sent'st it back to me:
Since when it grows, and smells, I swear,
  Not of itself, but thee.

BEN JONSON

It was a Beauty that I saw

FROM *THE NEW INN*

It was a beauty that I saw,
So pure, so perfect, as the frame
Of all the universe was lame,
To that one figure, could I draw,
Or give least line of it a law!

A skein of silk without a knot.
A fair march made without a halt!
A curious form without a fault.
A printed book without a blot.
All beauty, and without a spot!

BEN JONSON

BEN JONSON

Patrico's Song

FROM *THE METAMORPHOS'D GYPSIES*

The faery beam upon you
The stars to glister on you,
   A Moon of light
   In the Noon of night,
Till the firedrake hath o'er-gone you.

The wheel of fortune guide you,
The Boy with the bow beside you
   Run aye in the way
   Till the bird of day
And the luckier lot betide you.

To the old, long life and treasure,
To the young, all health and pleasure,
   To the fair, their face
   With eternal grace,
And the soul to be lov'd at leisure.

To the witty, all clear mirrors,
To the foolish, their dark errors,
   To the loving sprite
   A secure delight,
To the jealous his own false terrors.

BEN JONSON

JOHN WEBSTER

Cornelia's Song

FROM *THE WHITE DEVIL*

Call for the robin-redbreast and the wren,
Since o'er shady groves they hover,
And with leaves and flowers do cover
The friendless bodies of unburied men.
Call unto his funeral dole
The ant, the field-mouse, and the mole
To rear him hillocks, that shall keep him warm,
And (when gay tombs are robb'd) sustain no harm,
But keep the wolf far thence, that's foe to men,
For with his nails he'll dig them up agen.

JOHN WEBSTER

Care charming Sleep, Thou Easer of all Woes

FROM *THE TRAGEDY OF VALENTINIAN*

Care charming sleep, thou easer of all woes,
Brother to death, sweetly thy self dispose
On this afflicted Prince, fall like a Cloud
In gentle show'rs, give nothing that is loud,
Or painful to his slumbers; easy, sweet,
And as a purling stream, thou son of night,
Pass by his troubled senses; sing his pain
Like hollow murmuring wind, or silver rain,
Into this Prince gently, Oh gently slide,
And kiss him into slumbers like a Bride.

JOHN FLETCHER

Orpheus with his Lute *

FROM *KING HENRY VIII*

Orpheus with his lute made trees
And the mountain tops that freeze
   Bow themselves, when he did sing:
To his music plants and flowers
Ever sprung; as sun and showers
   There had made a lasting spring.

Every thing that heard him play,
Even the billows of the sea,
   Hung their heads, and then lay by.
In sweet music is such art,
Killing care and grief of heart
   Fall asleep, or hearing, die.

JOHN FLETCHER

* Written either by John Fletcher or William Shakespeare.

The Fairies' Farewell; or, God-a-Mercy Will

Farewell, rewards and Fairies,
Good housewives now may say,
For now foul sluts in Dairies
Do fare as well as they.
And though they sweep their hearths no less
Than maids were wont to do,
Yet who of late for cleanliness,
Finds Sixpence in her shoe?

. . . . .

At morning and at evening both,
You merry were and glad,
So little care of sleep or sloth
These pretty Ladies had;
When *Tom* came home from labour,
Or *Cisse* to milking rose,
Then merrily merrily went their Tabor,
And nimbly went their Toes.

Witness those rings and roundelays
Of theirs, which yet remain,
Were footed in Queen Mary's days
On many a grassy plain;
But since of late, *Elizabeth*,
And later *James* came in,
They never danced on any heath
As when the time hath been. . . .

RICHARD CORBET

Song

Fain would I change that note
　　To which fond Love hath charmed me
Long, long to sing by rote,
　　Fancying that that harmed me.
Yet when this thought doth come,
Love is the perfect sum
　　Of all delight,
I have no other choice
Either for pen or voice
　　To sing or write.

O Love, they wrong thee much
　　That say thy sweet is bitter
When thy rich fruit is such
　　As nothing can be sweeter.
Fair house of joy and bliss,
Where truest pleasure is,
　　I do adore thee.
I know thee what thou art,
I serve thee with my heart,
　　And fall before thee.

TOBIAS HUME

For the Baptist

The last and greatest Herald of Heaven's King,
Girt with rough skins, hies to the Deserts wild,
Among the savage brood the woods forth bring,
Which he than Man more harmless found and mild:
His food was Blossoms, and what young doth spring,
With Honey that from virgin Hives distil'd;
Parched Body, hollow Eyes, some uncouth thing
Made him appear, long since from Earth exiled.
There burst he forth; All ye, whose Hopes rely
On God, with me amidst these Deserts mourn,
Repent, repent, and from old errors turn.
Who listened to his voice, obey'd his cry?
  Only the Echoes which he made relent,
   Ring from their Marble Caves, repent, repent.

WILLIAM DRUMMOND

To the Virgins, to make much of Time

  Gather ye rosebuds while ye may,
    Old Time is still a-flying:
  And this same flower that smiles to-day,
    To-morrow will be dying.

  The glorious Lamp of Heaven, the Sun,
    The higher he's a-getting,
  The sooner will his race be run,
    And nearer he's to setting.

That Age is best which is the first,
   When Youth and Blood are warmer;
But being spent, the worse, and worst
   Times still succeed the former.

Then be not coy, but use your time;
   And while ye may, go marry:
For having lost but once your prime,
   You may for ever tarry.

ROBERT HERRICK

Delight in Disorder

A sweet disorder in the dress
Kindles in clothes a wantonness:
A Lawn about the shoulders thrown
Into a fine distraction:
An erring Lace, which here and there

Enthralls the Crimson Stomacher:
A Cuff neglectful, and thereby
Ribbands to flow confusedly:
A winning wave (deserving Note)
In the tempestuous petticoat:
A careless shoe-string, in whose tie
I see a wild civility:
Do more bewitch me, than when Art
Is too precise in every part.

ROBERT HERRICK

The Night Piece, to Julia

Her Eyes the Glow-worm lend thee,
The Shooting Stars attend thee
   And the Elves also,
   Whose little eyes glow,
Like the sparks of fire, befriend thee.

No *Will-o'-th'-Wisp* mis-light thee;
Nor Snake, or Slow-worm bite thee:
   But on, on thy way
   Not making a stay,
Since Ghost there's none to affright thee.

Let not the dark thee cumber;
What though the Moon does slumber?
   The Stars of the night
   Will lend thee their light,
Like Tapers clear without number.

Then Julia let me woo thee,
Thus, thus to come unto me:
   And when I shall meet
   Thy silvery feet,
My soul I'll pour into thee.

ROBERT HERRICK

On Zacheus

Me thinks, I see, with what a busie hast,
Zacheus climb'd the Tree: But, O, how fast,
How full of speed, canst thou imagine (when
Our *Saviour* call'd) he powder'd downe agen!
He ne're made *tryall* if the boughes were sound,
Or rotten; nor how far 'twas to the ground:
There was no danger fear'd; At such a Call,
Hee'l venture nothing, that dare feare a fall;
Needs must he downe by such a *Spirit* driven;
Nor could he fall, unless he fell to *Heaven*:
Down came *Zacheus*, ravisht from the Tree;
Bird that was shot ne're dropt so quicke as he.

FRANCIS QUARLES

Like to the Damask Rose

Like to the Damask Rose you see,
Or like the blossome on the tree,
Or like the dainty flower of May,
Or like the morning to the day,
Or like the Sunne, or like the shade,
Or like the Gourd which Jonas had;
   Even such is man, whose thred is spunn,
   Drawne out and cut, and so is done.

The Rose withers, the blossome blasteth,
The flower fades, the morning hasteth:
The Sunne sets, the shadow flies,
The Gourd consumes, and man he dies.

Like to the blaze of fond delight;
Or like a morning cleare and bright;
Or like a frost, or like a showre;
Or like the pride of Babel's Tower;
Or like the hower that guides the Time;
Or like to beauty in her prime;
   Even such is man, whose glory lends
   His life a blaze or two, and ends.

Delights vanish; the morne o'ercasteth,
The frost breaks, the shower hasteth;
The towre falls, the hower spends;
The beauty fades, and man's life ends.

FRANCIS QUARLES

Sic Vita

Like to the falling of a Star;
Or as the flights of Eagles are;
Or like the fresh spring's gaudy hue;
Or silver drops of morning dew;
Or like a wind that chafes the flood;
Or bubbles which on water stood;
Even such is man, whose borrow'd light
Is straight call'd in, and paid to-night.

The Wind blows out; the Bubble dies;
The Spring entomb'd in Autumn lies;
The Dew dries up; the Star is shot;
The Flight is past; and Man forgot.

HENRY KING, Bishop of Chichester

Easter

I got me flowers to strew Thy way,
I got me boughs off many a tree,
But Thou wast up by break of day,
And brought'st Thy sweets along with Thee.

The sunne arising in the East,
Though he give light, and th'East perfume,
If they should offer to contest
With Thy arising, they presume.

Can there be any day but this,
Though many sunnes to shine endeavour?
We count three hundred, but we misse:
There is but one, and that one ever.

GEORGE HERBERT

Love

Love bade me welcome: yet my soul drew back,
    Guilty of dust and sin.
But quick-ey'd Love, observing me grow slack
    From my first entrance in,
Drew nearer to me, sweetly questioning
    If I lack'd any thing.

'A guest,' I answer'd, 'worthy to be here':
    Love said, 'You shall be he.'
'I, the unkind, ungrateful? Ah my dear,
    I cannot look on Thee.'
Love took my hand, and smiling did reply,
    'Who made the eyes but I?'
'Truth Lord; but I have marr'd them; let my shame
    Go where it doth deserve.'

'And know you not,' says Love, 'Who bore the blame?'
  'My dear, then I will serve.'
'You must sit down,' says Love, 'and taste My meat.'
  So I did sit and eat.

GEORGE HERBERT

He that loves a Rosy Cheek

He that loves a Rosy cheek,
  Or a Coral lip admires,
Or from Star-like eyes doth seek
  Fuel to maintain his fires;
As old Time makes these decay,
So his flames must waste away.

But a smooth and steadfast mind,
  Gentle thoughts, and calm desires,
Hearts with equal love combined,
  Kindle never-dying fires,
Where these are not, I despise
Lovely cheeks, or lips, or eyes.

No tears, *Celia*, now shall win,
   My resolved heart, to return;
I have searched thy soul within,
   And find nought, but pride, and scorn;
I have learned thy arts, and now
Can disdain as much as thou.
Some power, in my revenge convey
That love to her, I cast away.

THOMAS CAREW

L'Allegro

Hence loathèd Melancholy,
   Of *Cerberus*, and blackest midnight born,
In *Stygian* Cave forlorn
   'Mongst horrid shapes, and shrieks, and sights unholy,
Find out some uncouth cell,
   Where brooding darkness spreads his jealous wings,
And the night-Raven sings;
   There under *Ebon* shades, and low-brow'd Rocks,
As ragged as thy Locks,
   In dark *Cimmerian* desert ever dwell.
But come thou Goddess fair and free,
In Heav'n yclept *Euphrosyne*,
And by men, heart-easing Mirth,
Whom lovely *Venus* at a birth
With two sister Graces more
To Ivy-crownèd *Bacchus* bore;

Or whether (as some sager sing)
The frolic Wind that breathes the Spring,
Zephir with *Aurora* playing,
As he met her once a-Maying,
There on Beds of Violets blue,
And fresh-blown Roses wash'd in dew,
Fill'd her with thee a daughter fair,
So bucksome, blithe, and debonair.
Haste thee nymph, and bring with thee
Jest and youthful Jollity,
Quips and Cranks, and wanton Wiles,
Nods, and Becks, and Wreathèd Smiles,
Such as hang on *Hebe's* cheek,
And love to live in dimple sleek;
Sport that wrinkled Care derides,
And Laughter holding both his sides.
Come, and trip it as ye go
On the light fantastic toe,
And in thy right hand lead with thee,
The Mountain Nymph, sweet Liberty;
And if I give thee honour due,
Mirth, admit me of thy crew
To live with her, and live with thee,
In unreprovèd pleasures free;
To hear the Lark begin his flight,
And singing startle the dull night,
From his watch-tower in the skies,
Till the dappled dawn doth rise;
Then to come in spite of sorrow,
And at my window bid good morrow,
Through the Sweet-Briar, or the Vine,
Or the twisted Eglantine.
While the Cock with lively din,

Scatters the rear of darkness thin,
And to the stack, or the Barn door,
Stoutly struts his Dames before,
Oft listening how the Hounds and horn
Cheerly rouse the slumbring morn,
From the side of some Hoar Hill,
Through the high wood echoing shrill.
Some time walking not unseen
By Hedge-row Elms, on Hillocks green,
Right against the Eastern gate,
Where the great Sun begins his state,
Robed in flames, and Amber light,
The clouds in thousand Liveries dight.
While the Plowman near at hand,
Whistles o'er the Furrow'd Land,
And the Milkmaid singeth blithe,
And the Mower whets his scythe,
And every Shepherd tells his tale
Under the Hawthorn in the dale.
Straight mine eye hath caught new pleasures
Whilst the Landscape round it measures,
Russet Lawns, and Fallows Gray,
Where the nibbling flocks do stray,
Mountains on whose barren breast
The labouring clouds do often rest:
Meadows trim with Daisies pied,
Shallow Brooks, and Rivers wide.
Towers, and Battlements it sees
Bosom'd high in tufted Trees,
Where perhaps some beauty lies,
The Cynosure of neighbouring eyes.
Hard by, a Cottage chimney smokes,
From betwixt two aged Oaks,

Where *Corydon* and *Thyrsis* met,
Are at their savoury dinner set
Of Herbs, and other Country Messes,
Which the neat-handed *Phillis* dresses;
And then in haste her Bower she leaves,
With *Thestylis* to bind the Sheaves;
Or if the earlier season lead
To the tann'd Haycock in the Mead,
Sometimes with secure delight
The up-land Hamlets will invite,
When the merry Bells ring round,
And the jocund rebecks sound
To many a youth, and many a maid,
Dancing in the Chequer'd shade;
And young and old come forth to play
On a Sunshine Holyday,
Till the live-long day-light fail,
Then to the Spicy Nut-brown Ale,
With stories told of many a feat,
How *Faery Mab* the junkets eat,
She was pinch'd, and pull'd, she said,
And he by Friar's Lanthorn led
Tells how the drudging *Goblin* sweat,
To earn his Cream-bowl duly set,
When in one night, ere glimpse of morn,
His shadowy Flail hath thresh'd the Corn
That ten day-labourers could not end,
Then lies him down the Lubber Fiend.
And stretch'd out all the Chimney's length,
Basks at the fire his hairy strength;
And Crop-full out of doors he flings,
Ere the first Cock his Matin rings.
Thus done the Tales, to bed they creep,

By whispering Winds soon lull'd asleep.
Towered Cities please us then,
And the busy hum of men,
Where throngs of Knights and Barons bold,
In weeds of Peace high triumphs hold,
With store of Ladies, whose bright eyes
Rain influence, and judge the prize
Of Wit, or Arms, while both contend
To win her Grace, whom all commend.
There let *Hymen* oft appear
In Saffron robe, with Taper clear,
And pomp, and feast, and revelry,
With mask, and antique Pageantry,
Such sights as youthful Poets dream
On Summer eves by haunted stream.
Then to the well-trod stage anon,
If *Jonson's* learned Sock be on,
Or sweetest *Shakespeare*, Fancy's child,
Warble his native Wood-notes wild,
And ever against eating Cares,
Lap me in soft *Lydian* Airs,
Married to immortal verse
Such as the meeting soul may pierce
In notes, with many a winding bout
Of linkèd sweetness long drawn out,
With wanton heed, and giddy cunning,
The melting voice through mazes running;
Untwisting all the chains that tie
The hidden soul of harmony.
That *Orpheus'* self may heave his head
From golden slumber on a bed
Of heap'd *Elysian* flowers, and hear
Such strains as would have won the ear

Of *Pluto*, to have quite set free
His half regain'd *Eurydice*.
These delights, if thou canst give,
Mirth, with thee I mean to live.

JOHN MILTON

On His Blindness

When I consider how my light is spent,
  Ere half my days, in this dark world and wide,
  And that one Talent which is death to hide,
  Lodg'd with me useless, though my Soul more bent
To serve therewith my Maker, and present
  My true account, lest he returning chide,
  Doth God exact day-labour, light denied?
  I fondly ask; But patience to prevent
That murmur, soon replies; God doth not need
  Either man's work or his own gifts: who best
Bear his mild yoke, they serve him best: his State
Is Kingly. Thousands at his bidding speed
  And post o'er Land and Ocean without rest:
  They also serve who only stand and wait.

JOHN MILTON

On Shakespeare

What needs my Shakespeare for his honoured bones
The labour of an age in pilèd stones?
Or that his hallowed reliques should be hid
Under a star-ypointing pyramid?
Dear son of memory, great heir of fame,
What need'st thou such weak witness of thy name?
Thou in our wonder and astonishment
Hast built thyself a live-long monument.
For whilst to th'shame of slow-endeavouring art,
Thy easy numbers flow, and that each heart
Hath from the leaves of thy unvalued book
Those Delphic lines with deep impression took,
Then thou, our fancy of itself bereaving,
Dost make us marble with too much conceiving;
And so sepulchred in such pomp dost lie
That kings for such a tomb would wish to die.

JOHN MILTON

Time

How soon hath Time the subtle thief of youth,
    Stol'n on his wing my three and twentieth year!
    My hasting days fly on with full career,
    But my late spring no bud or blossom shew'th
Perhaps my semblance might deceive the truth,
    That I to manhood am arrived so near,
    And inward ripeness doth much less appear,

That some more timely-happy spirits endu'th.
Yet be it less or more, or soon or slow,
  It shall be still in strictest measure ev'n,
  To that same lot, however mean, or high,
Toward which Time leads me, and the will of Heav'n;
  All is, if I have grace to use it so,
  As ever in my great Task-Master's eye.

JOHN MILTON

Il Penseroso

Hence vain deluding joys,
  The brood of folly without father bred,
How little you bestead,
  Or fill the fixèd mind with all your toys ;
Dwell in some idle brain,
  And fancies fond with gaudy shapes possess,
As thick and numberless
  As the gay motes that people the Sun Beams,
Or likest hovering dreams
  The fickle Pensioners of *Morpheus'* train.
But hail thou Goddess, sage and holy,
Hail divinest Melancholy,
Whose Saintly visage is too bright
To hit the Sense of human sight ;

And therefore to our weaker view,
O'erlaid with black, staid Wisdom's hue.
Black, but such as in esteem,
Prince *Memnon's* sister might beseem,
Or that Starr'd *Ethiop* Queen that strove
To set her beauties' praise above
The Sea Nymphs, and their powers offended.
Yet thou art higher far descended,
Thee bright-hair'd *Vesta* long of yore,
To solitary *Saturn* bore ;
His daughter she (in *Saturn's* reign,
Such mixture was not held a stain)
Oft in glimmering Bowers, and glades
He met her, and in secret shades
Of woody *Ida's* inmost grove,
While yet there was no fear of *Jove.*
Come pensive Nun, devout and pure,
Sober, steadfast, and demure,
All in a robe of darkest grain,
Flowing with majestic train,
And sable stole of *Cipres* Lawn,
Over thy decent shoulders drawn.
Come, but keep thy wonted state,
With even step, and musing gait,
And looks commercing with the skies,
Thy rapt soul sitting in thine eyes :
There held in holy passion still,
Forget thyself to Marble, till
With a sad Leaden downward cast,
Thou fix them on the earth as fast.
And join with thee calm Peace, and Quiet,
Spare Fast, that oft with gods doth diet,
And hears the Muses in a ring,

Aye round about *Jove's* Altar sing.
And add to these retired Leisure,
That in trim Gardens takes his pleasure ;
But first, and chiefest, with thee bring,
Him that yon soars on golden wing,
Guiding the fiery-wheelèd throne,
The Cherub Contemplation,
And the mute Silence hist along,
'Less *Philomel* will deign a Song,
In her sweetest, saddest plight,
Smoothing the rugged brow of night,
While *Cynthia* checks her Dragon yoke,
Gently o'er th' accustom'd Oak ;
Sweet Bird that shunn'st the noise of folly,
Most musical, most melancholy !
Thee Chauntress oft the Woods among,
I woo to hear thy evensong ;
And missing thee, I walk unseen
On the dry smooth-shaven Green,
To behold the wandering Moon,
Riding near her highest noon,
Like one that had been led astray
Through the Heav'n's wide pathless way,
And oft, as if her head she bow'd,
Stooping through a fleecy cloud.
Oft on a Plat of rising ground,
I hear the far-off *Curfeu* sound,
Over some wide-water'd shore,
Swinging slow with sullen roar ;
Or if the Air will not permit,
Some still removèd place will fit,
Where glowing Embers through the room
Teach light to counterfeit a gloom,

Far from all resort of mirth,
Save the Cricket on the hearth,
Or the Bellman's drowsy charm,
To bless the doors from nightly harm :
Or let my Lamp at midnight hour,
Be seen in some high lonely Tower,
Where I may oft out-watch the *Bear*,
With thrice great *Hermes*, or unsphere
The spirit of *Plato* to unfold
What Worlds, or what vast Regions hold
The immortal mind that hath forsook
Her mansion in this fleshly nook :
And of those *Demons* that are found
In fire, air, flood, or under ground,
Whose power hath a true consent
With Planet, or with Element.
Some time let Gorgeous Tragedy
In Scepter'd Pall come sweeping by,
Presenting *Thebes*, or *Pelops'* line,
Or the tale of *Troy* divine.
Or what (though rare) of later age,
Ennobled hath the Buskin'd stage.
But, O sad Virgin, that thy power
Might raise *Musæus* from his bower,
Or bid the soul of *Orpheus* sing
Such notes as warbled to the string,
Drew Iron tears down *Pluto's* cheek,
And made Hell grant what Love did seek.
Or call up him that left half told
The story of *Cambuscan* bold,
Of *Camball*, and of *Algarsife*,
And who had *Canacé* to wife,
That own'd the virtuous Ring and Glass

And of the wondrous Horse of Brass,
On which the *Tartar* King did ride ;
And if aught else, great *Bards* beside,
In sage and solemn tunes have sung,
Of Turneys and of Trophies hung ;
Of Forests, and enchantments drear,
Where more is meant than meets the ear.
Thus night oft see me in thy pale career,
Till civil-suited Morn appear,
Not trick'd and frounc'd as she was wont,
With the Attic Boy to hunt,
But kercheft in a comely Cloud,
While rocking Winds are Piping loud,
Or usher'd with a shower still,
When the gust hath blown his fill,
Ending on the rustling Leaves,
With minute drops from off the Eaves.
And when the Sun begins to fling
His flaring beams, me, Goddess, bring
To archèd walks of twilight groves,
And shadows brown that *Sylvan* loves
Of Pine, or monumental Oak,
Where the rude Axe with heavèd stroke,
Was never heard the Nymphs to daunt,
Or fright them from their hallow'd haunt.
There in close covert by some Brook,
Where no profaner eye may look,
Hide me from Day's garish eye,
While the Bee with honeyed thigh,
That at her flowery work doth sing,
And the Waters murmuring
With such consort as they keep,
Entice the dewy-feather'd Sleep ;

And let some strange mysterious dream,
Wave at his Wings in Airy stream,
Of lively portraiture display'd,
Softly on my eye-lids laid.
And as I wake, sweet music breathe
Above, about, or underneath,
Sent by some spirit to mortals good,
Or th'unseen Genius of the Wood.
But let my due feet never fail,
To walk the studious Cloisters pale,
And love the high embowéd Roof,
With antic Pillars massy proof,
And storied Windows richly dight,
Casting a dim religious light.
There let the pealing Organ blow,
To the full-voicèd Quire below,
In Service high, and Anthems clear,
As may with sweetness, through mine ear,
Dissolve me into ecstasies,
And bring all Heav'n before mine eyes.
And may at last my weary age
Find out the peaceful hermitage,
The Hairy Gown and Mossy Cell,
Where I may sit and rightly spell
Of every Star that Heav'n doth shew,
And every Herb that sips the dew ;
Till old experience do attain
To something like Prophetic strain.
These pleasures *Melancholy* give,
And I with thee will choose to live.

JOHN MILTON

Go Lovely Rose

Go lovely Rose—
Tell her, that wastes her time and me,
That now she knows,
When I resemble her to thee,
How sweet and fair she seems to be.

Tell her that's young,
And shuns to have her graces spied,
That hadst thou sprung
In deserts where no men abide,
Thou must have uncommended died.

Small is the worth
Of beauty from the light retir'd:
Bid her come forth,
Suffer her self to be desir'd,
And not blush so to be admir'd.

Then die, that she
The common fate of all things rare
May read in thee,
How small a part of time they share,
That are so wondrous sweet and fair.

EDMUND WALLER

The Constant Lover

Out upon it, I have loved
  Three whole days together!
And am like to love three more,
  If it prove fair weather.

Time shall moult away his wings
  Ere he shall discover
In the whole wide world again
  Such a constant lover.

But the spite on 't is, no praise
  Is due at all to me:
Love with me had made no stays,
  Had it any been but she.

Had it any been but she,
  And that very face,
There had been at least ere this
  A dozen dozen in her place.

SIR JOHN SUCKLING

To Althea, from Prison

When Love with unconfinéd wings
   Hovers within my Gates;
And my divine *Althea* brings
   To whisper at the Grates:
When I lie tangled in her hair,
   And fetter'd to her eye;
The *Birds*, that wanton in the Air,
   Know no such Liberty.

When flowing Cups run swiftly round
   With no allaying *Thames*,
Our careless heads with Roses bound,
   Our hearts with Loyal Flames;
When thirsty grief in Wine we steep,
   When Healths and draughts go free,
Fishes that tipple in the Deep,
   Know no such Liberty.

When (like committed Linnets) I
   With shriller throat shall sing
The sweetness, Mercy, Majesty,
   And glories of my King;
When I shall voice aloud, how Good
   He is, how Great should be;
Enlargéd Winds that curl the Flood,
   Know no such Liberty.

Stone Walls do not a Prison make,
   Nor Iron bars a Cage;
Minds innocent and quiet take

That for an Hermitage;
   If I have freedom in my Love,
     And in my soul am free;
   Angels alone, that soar above,
     Enjoy such Liberty.

RICHARD LOVELACE

Birds: MS. later altered to *Gods*

To Lucasta, going to the Wars

Tell me not, Sweet, I am unkind,
   That from the Nunnery
Of thy chaste breast and quiet mind,
   To War and Arms I fly.

True; a new Mistress now I chase,
   The first Foe in the Field;
And with a stronger Faith embrace
   A Sword, a Horse, a Shield.

Yet this Inconstancy is such,
    As thou too shalt adore;
I could not love thee, Dear, so much,
    Lov'd I not Honour more.

RICHARD LOVELACE

To his Coy Mistress

Had we but World enough, and Time,
This coyness, Lady, were no crime.
We would sit down, and think which way
To walk, and pass our long Love's Day.
Thou by the *Indian Ganges'* side
Shouldst Rubies find: I by the Tide
Of *Humber* would complain. I would
Love you ten years before the Flood:

And you should if you please refuse
Till the Conversion of the *Jews*.
My vegetable Love should grow
Vaster than Empires, and more slow.
An hundred years should go to praise
Thine Eyes, and on thy Forehead Gaze.
Two hundred to adore each Breast:
But thirty thousand to the rest.
An Age at least to every part,
And the last Age should show your Heart.
For Lady you deserve this State;
Nor would I love at lower rate.
    But at my back I always hear
Time's wingèd Chariot hurrying near:
And yonder all before us lie
Deserts of vast Eternity.
Thy Beauty shall no more be found;
Nor, in thy marble Vault, shall sound
My echoing Song: then Worms shall try
That long-preserv'd Virginity:
And your quaint Honour turn to dust;
And into ashes all my Lust.
The Grave's a fine and private place,
But none I think do there embrace.
    Now therefore, while the youthful hue
Sits on thy skin like morning dew,
And while thy willing Soul transpires
At every pore with instant Fires,
Now let us sport us while we may;
And now, like amorous birds of prey,
Rather at once our Time devour,
Than languish in his slow-chapt power.
Let us roll all our Strength and all

Our sweetness up into one Ball:
And tear our Pleasures with rough strife,
Thorough the Iron gates of Life.
Thus, though we cannot make our Sun
Stand still, yet we will make him run.

ANDREW MARVELL

Preparations

From a MS. at Christ Church, Oxford

Yet if His Majesty, our sovereign lord,
Should of his own accord
Friendly himself invite,
And say 'I'll be your guest to-morrow night,'
How should we stir ourselves, call and command
All hands to work! 'Let no man idle stand!

'Set me fine Spanish tables in the hall:
See they be fitted all;
Let there be room to eat
And order taken that there want no meat.
See every sconce and candlestick made bright,
That without tapers they may give a light.

'Look to the presence: are the carpets spread,
The dazie o'er the head,
The cushions in the chairs,
And all the candles lighted on the stairs?
Perfume the chambers, and in any case
Let each man give attendance in his place!'

Thus, if a king were coming, would we do;
And 'twere good reason too;
For 'tis a duteous thing
To show all honour to an earthly king,
And after all our travail and our cost,
So he be pleased, to think no labour lost.

But at the coming of the King of Heaven
All's set at six and seven;
We wallow in our sin,
Christ cannot find a chamber in the inn.
We entertain Him always like a stranger,
And, as at first, still lodge Him in the Manger.

ANONYMOUS

dazie = dais; the canopy over a throne.

Peace

My Soul, there is a Country
    Far beyond the stars,
Where stands a wingèd sentry
    All skilful in the wars,

There above noise, and danger,
   Sweet peace sits crown'd with smiles.
And one born in a Manger
   Commands the Beauteous files,
He is thy gracious friend,
   And (O my Soul awake!)
Did in pure Love descend
   To die here for thy sake;
If thou canst get but thither,
   There grows the flower of peace,
The Rose that cannot wither,
   Thy fortress, and thy ease;
Leave then thy foolish ranges;
   For none can thee secure,
But one, who never changes,
   Thy God, thy life, thy Cure.

HENRY VAUGHAN

A Song for St. Cecilia's Day

November 22, 1687

From harmony, from heavenly harmony,
   This universal frame began;
  When nature underneath a heap
   Of jarring atoms lay,

And could not heave her head,
The tuneful voice was heard from high,
   'Arise, ye more than dead!'

Then cold and hot and moist and dry
   In order to their stations leap,
     And Music's power obey.
From harmony, from heavenly harmony,
   This universal frame began:
   From harmony to harmony
Through all the compass of the notes it ran,
The diapason closing full in Man.

What passion cannot Music raise and quell?
   When Jubal struck the chorded shell,
  His listening brethren stood around,
   And, wondering, on their faces fell
  To worship that celestial sound:
Less than a God they thought there could not dwell
   Within the hollow of that shell,
   That spoke so sweetly, and so well.
What passion cannot Music raise and quell?

   The trumpet's loud clangour
     Excites us to arms
   With shrill notes of anger
     And mortal alarms.
   The double double double beat
     Of the thundering drum
     Cries, Hark! the foes come;
Charge, charge, 'tis too late to retreat.

The soft complaining flute
In dying notes discovers
The woes of hopeless lovers,
Whose dirge is whispered by the warbling lute.

Sharp violins proclaim
Their jealous pangs and desperation,
Fury, frantic indignation,
Depth of pains and height of passion,
For the fair, disdainful dame.

But O, what art can teach,
What human voice can reach
The sacred organ's praise?
Notes inspiring holy love,
Notes that wing their heavenly ways
To mend the choirs above.

Orpheus could lead the savage race,
And trees unrooted left their place,
Sequacious of the lyre;
But bright Cecilia rais'd the wonder higher:
When to her organ vocal breath was given,
An angel heard, and straight appear'd
Mistaking Earth for Heaven.

GRAND CHORUS

As from the power of sacred lays
The spheres began to move,
And sung the great Creator's praise
To all the Blest above;

So, when the last and dreadful hour
This crumbling pageant shall devour,
The trumpet shall be heard on high,
The dead shall live, the living die,
And Music shall untune the sky!

JOHN DRYDEN

Hampton Court

FROM *THE RAPE OF THE LOCK*

Close by those meads, for ever crown'd with flow'rs,
Where Thames with pride surveys his rising tow'rs,
There stands a structure of majestic frame,
Which from the neighb'ring Hampton takes its name.
Here Britain's statesmen oft the fall foredoom
Of foreign tyrants, and of nymphs at home;
Here thou, great ANNA! whom three realms obey,
Dost sometimes counsel take—and sometimes Tea.

Hither the heroes and the nymphs resort,
To taste awhile the pleasures of a Court;
In various talk th' instructive hours they past,
Who gave the ball, or paid the visit last;
One speaks the glory of the British Queen,
And one describes a charming Indian screen;
A third interprets motions, looks, and eyes;
At ev'ry word a reputation dies.
Snuff, or the fan, supply each pause of chat,
With singing, laughing, ogling, and all that.

ALEXANDER POPE

The Ombre Party

FROM *THE RAPE OF THE LOCK*

For lo! the board with cups and spoons is crowned,
The berries crackle, and the mill turns round;
On shining altars of Japan they raise
The silver lamp; the fiery spirits blaze:
From silver spouts the grateful liquors glide,
While China's earth receives the smoking tide:
At once they gratify their scent and taste,
And frequent cups prolong the rich repast.
Straight hover round the fair her airy band;
Some, as she sipped, the fuming liquor fanned,

Some o'er her lap their careful plumes displayed,
Trembling, and conscious of the rich brocade.
Coffee (which makes the politician wise,
And see through all things with his half-shut eyes)
Sent up in vapours to the Baron's brain
New stratagems, the radiant lock to gain.
Ah cease, rash youth! desist ere 'tis too late,
Fear the just Gods, and think of Scylla's fate!
Changed to a bird, and sent to flit in air,
She dearly pays for Nisus' injured hair!

But when to mischief mortals bend their will,
How soon they find fit instruments of ill!
Just then, Clarissa drew with tempting grace
A two-edged weapon from her shining case:
So ladies in romance assist their knight,
Present the spear, and arm him for the fight.
He takes the gift with reverence, and extends
The little engine on his fingers' ends;
This just behind Belinda's neck he spread,
As o'er the fragrant steams she bends her head.
Swift to the lock a thousand sprites repair,
A thousand wings, by turns, blow back the hair;
And thrice they twitched the diamond in her ear;
Thrice she looked back, and thrice the foe drew near.
Just in that instant, anxious Ariel sought
The close recesses of the virgin's thought;
As on the nosegay in her breast reclined,
He watched the ideas rising in her mind,
Sudden he viewed, in spite of all her art,
An earthly lover lurking at her heart.
Amazed, confused, he found his power expired,
Resigned to fate, and with a sigh retired.

The peer now spreads the glittering forfex wide,

To inclose the lock; now joins it, to divide.
Even then, before the fatal engine closèd,
A wretched sylph too fondly interposed;
Fate urged the shears, and cut the sylph in twain,
(But airy substance soon unites again)
The meeting points the sacred hair dissever
From the fair head, for ever, and for ever!

 Then flashed the living lightning from her eyes,
And screams of horror rend the affrighted skies.
Not louder shrieks to pitying heaven are cast,
When husbands, or when lap-dogs breathe their last;
Or when rich China vessels fallen from high,
In glittering dust and painted fragments lie!

 'Let wreaths of triumph now my temples twine,'
(The victor cried) 'the glorious prize is mine!'
While fish in streams, or birds delight in air,
Or in a coach and six the British fair,
As long as Atalantis shall be read,
Or the small pillow grace a lady's bed,
While visits shall be paid on solemn days,
When numerous wax-lights in bright order blaze,
While nymphs take treats, or assignations give,
So long my honour, name, and praise shall live!
What time would spare, from steel receives its date,
And monuments, like men, submit to fate!
Steel could the labour of the Gods destroy,
And strike to dust the imperial towers of Troy;
Steel could the works of mortal pride confound,
And hew triumphal arches to the ground.
What wonder then, fair nymph! thy hairs should feel
The conquering force of unresisted steel?

ALEXANDER POPE

ALEXANDER POPE

Where'er you walk

FROM *SUMMER*

Where'er you walk, cool gales shall fan the glade ;
Trees, where you sit, shall crowd into a shade ;
Where'er you tread, the blushing flowers shall rise,
And all things flourish where you turn your eyes.
Oh ! how I long with you to pass my days,
Invoke the Muses, and resound your praise !
Your praise the birds shall chant in ev'ry grove,
And winds shall waft it to the pow'rs above,
But would you sing, and rival Orpheus' strain,
The wond'ring forests soon should dance again ;
The moving mountains hear the powerful call,
And headlong streams hang list'ning in their fall !

But see, the shepherds shun the noonday heat,
The lowing herds to murm'ring brooks retreat,
To closer shades the panting flocks remove ;
Ye Gods ! and is there no relief for Love ?
But soon the sun with milder rays descends
To the cool ocean, where his journey ends.
On me love's fiercer flames for ever prey,
By night he scorches, as he burns by day.

ALEXANDER POPE

On a Certain Lady at Court

I know the thing that's most uncommon ;
    (Envy be silent and attend !)
I know a Reasonable woman,
    Handsome and witty, yet a Friend.

Not warp'd by Passion, aw'd by Rumour,
    Not grave thro' Pride, or gay thro' Folly,
An equal Mixture of good Humour,
    And sensible soft Melancholy.

'Has she no Faults then (Envy says) Sir ?'
    Yes she has one, I must aver :
When all the world conspires to praise her,
    The woman's deaf, and does not hear.

ALEXANDER POPE

The Bull

FROM *THE SEASONS*

Through all his lusty veins
The bull, deep-scorched, the raging passion feels.
Of pasture sick, and negligent of food,
Scarce seen he wades among the yellow broom,
While o'er his ample sides the rambling sprays
Luxuriant shoot; or through the mazy wood
Dejected wanders, nor the enticing bud
Crops, though it presses on his careless sense.
And oft, in jealous maddening fancy wrapt,
He seeks the fight; and, idly butting, feigns
His rival gored in every knotty trunk.
Him should he meet, the bellowing war begins:
Their eyes flash fury; to the hollowed earth,
Whence the sand flies, they mutter bloody deeds,
And, groaning deep, the impetuous battle mix:
While the fair heifer, balmy-breathing near,
Stands kindling up their rage. The trembling steed,
With this hot impulse seized in every nerve,
Nor heeds the rein, nor hears the sounding thong;
Blows are not felt; but, tossing high his head,
And by the well-known joy to distant plains
Attracted strong, all wild he bursts away;
O'er rocks, and woods, and craggy mountains flies;
And, neighing, on the aerial summit takes
The exciting gale; then, steep-descending, cleaves
The headlong torrents foaming down the hills,
Even where the madness of the straitened stream
Turns in black eddies round: such is the force
With which his frantic heart and sinews swell.

JAMES THOMSON

Long-expected one and twenty

Long-expected one and twenty
Ling'ring year at last is flown ;
Pomp and Pleasure, Pride and Plenty
Great Sir John, are all your own.

Loosen'd from the Minor's tether,
Free to mortgage or to sell,
Wild as wind, and light as feather
Bid the Slaves of thrift farewell.

Call the Bettys, Kates, and Jennys
Ev'ry name that laughs at Care,
Lavish of your Grandsire's guineas,
Show the Spirit of an heir.

All that prey on vice and folly
Joy to see their quarry fly,
Here the Gamester light and jolly,
There the Lender grave and sly.

Wealth, Sir John, was made to wander,
Let it wander as it will;
See the Jockey, see the Pander,
Bid them come, and take their fill.

When the bonny Blade carouses,
Pockets full, and Spirits high,
What are acres ?   What are houses ?
Only dirt, or wet or dry.

SAMUEL JOHNSON

If the Guardian or the Mother
Tell the woes of wilful waste,
Scorn their counsel and their pother,
You can hang or drown at last.

SAMUEL JOHNSON

Elegy written in a Country Churchyard

The Curfew tolls the knell of parting day,
   The lowing herd wind slowly o'er the lea,
The plowman homeward plods his weary way,
   And leaves the world to darkness and to me.

Now fades the glimmering landscape on the sight,
   And all the air a solemn stillness holds,
Save where the beetle wheels his droning flight,
   And drowsy tinklings lull the distant folds;

Save that from yonder ivy-mantled tow'r
   The moping owl does to the moon complain

Of such as, wand'ring near her secret bow'r,
    Molest her ancient solitary reign.

Beneath those rugged elms, that yew-tree's shade,
    Where heaves the turf in many a mould'ring heap,
Each in his narrow cell for ever laid,
    The rude Forefathers of the hamlet sleep.

The breezy call of incense-breathing Morn,
    The swallow twitt'ring from the straw-built shed,
The cock's shrill clarion, or the echoing horn,
    No more shall rouse them from their lowly bed.

For them no more the blazing hearth shall burn,
    Or busy housewife ply her evening care:
No children run to lisp their sire's return,
    Or climb his knees the envied kiss to share.

Oft did the harvest to their sickle yield,
    Their furrow oft the stubborn glebe has broke;
How jocund did they drive their team afield!
    How bow'd the woods beneath their sturdy stroke!

Let not Ambition mock their useful toil,
    Their homely joys, and destiny obscure;
Nor Grandeur hear with a disdainful smile
    The short and simple annals of the poor.

The boast of heraldry, the pomp of pow'r,
    And all that beauty, all that wealth e'er gave,
Awaits alike th'inevitable hour.
    The paths of glory lead but to the grave.

Nor you, ye Proud, impute to These the fault,
  If Memory o'er their Tomb no Trophies raise,
Where through the long-drawn aisle and fretted vault
  The pealing anthem swells the note of praise.

Can storied urn or animated bust
  Back to its mansion call the fleeting breath?
Can Honour's voice provoke the silent dust,
  Or Flatt'ry soothe the dull cold ear of death?

Perhaps in this neglected spot is laid
  Some heart once pregnant with celestial fire;
Hands, that the rod of empire might have sway'd,
  Or waked to ecstasy the living lyre.

But Knowledge to their eyes her ample page
  Rich with the spoils of time did ne'er unroll:
Chill Penury repress'd their noble rage,
  And froze the genial current of the soul.

Full many a gem of purest ray serene
  The dark unfathom'd caves of ocean bear:
Full many a flower is born to blush unseen,
  And waste its sweetness on the desert air.

Some village Hampden, that with dauntless breast
  The little tyrant of his fields withstood;
Some mute inglorious Milton, here may rest,
  Some Cromwell guiltless of his country's blood.

Th'applause of list'ning senates to command,
  The threats of pain and ruin to despise,

To scatter plenty o'er a smiling land,
   And read their history in a nation's eyes—

Their lot forbade: nor circumscribed alone
   Their growing virtues, but their crimes confined;
Forbade to wade through slaughter to a throne,
   And shut the gates of mercy on mankind;

The struggling pangs of conscious truth to hide,
   To quench the blushes of ingenuous shame,
Or heap the shrine of Luxury and Pride
   With incense kindled at the Muse's flame.

Far from the madding crowd's ignoble strife,
   Their sober wishes never learn'd to stray;
Along the cool sequester'd vale of life
   They kept the noiseless tenor of their way.

Yet ev'n these bones from insult to protect
   Some frail memorial still erected nigh,
With uncouth rhymes and shapeless sculpture deck'd,
   Implores the passing tribute of a sigh.

Their name, their years, spelt by th'unletter'd Muse,
   The place of fame and elegy supply:
And many a holy text around she strews,
   That teach the rustic moralist to die.

For who, to dumb Forgetfulness a prey,
   This pleasing anxious being e'er resign'd,
Left the warm precincts of the cheerful day,
   Nor cast one longing lingering look behind?

On some fond breast the parting soul relies,
  Some pious drops the closing eye requires;
Ev'n from the tomb the voice of Nature cries,
  Ev'n in our Ashes live their wonted Fires.

For thee, who, mindful of th'unhonour'd dead,
  Dost in these lines their artless tale relate;
If chance, by lonely contemplation led,
  Some kindred spirit shall inquire thy fate,

Haply some hoary-headed swain may say,
  'Oft have we seen him at the peep of dawn
Brushing with hasty steps the dews away
  To meet the sun upon the upland lawn.

'There at the foot of yonder nodding beech
  That wreathes its old fantastic roots so high,
His listless length at noontide would he stretch,
  And pore upon the brook that babbles by.

'Hard by yon wood, now smiling as in scorn,
  Mutt'ring his wayward fancies he would rove,
Now drooping, woeful wan, like one forlorn,
  Or crazed with care, or cross'd in hopeless love.

'One morn I miss'd him on the custom'd hill,
  Along the heath, and near his fav'rite tree;
Another came; nor yet beside the rill,
  Nor up the lawn, nor at the wood was he;

'The next with dirges due in sad array
  Slow through the church-way path we saw him borne.

Approach and read (for thou canst read) the lay
    Graved on the stone beneath yon aged thorn.'

The Epitaph

Here rests his head upon the lap of Earth
    A Youth to Fortune and to Fame unknown.
Fair Science frown'd not on his humble birth,
    And Melancholy mark'd him for her own.

Large was his bounty, and his soul sincere,
    Heaven did a recompense as largely send;
He gave to Mis'ry all he had, a tear,
    He gain'd from Heaven ('twas all he wish'd) a friend.

No farther seek his merits to disclose,
    Or draw his frailties from their dread abode,
(There they alike in trembling hope repose,)
    The bosom of his Father and his God.

THOMAS GRAY

Ode to Evening

If aught of oaten stop, or pastoral song,
  May hope, chaste Eve, to soothe thy modest ear,
    Like thy own solemn springs,
    Thy springs and dying gales;

O nymph reserved, while now the bright-hair'd sun
Sits in yon western tent, whose cloudy skirts,
    With brede ethereal wove,
    O'erhang his wavy bed:

Now air is hush'd save where the weak-eyed bat
With short shrill shriek flits by on leathern wing,
    Or where the beetle winds
    His small but sullen horn,

As oft he rises, 'midst the twilight path
Against the pilgrim borne in heedless hum:
    Now teach me, maid composed,
    To breathe some soften'd strain,

Whose numbers, stealing through thy dark'ning vale,
May not unseemly with its stillness suit,
    As, musing slow, I hail
    Thy genial loved return!

For when thy folding-star arising shows
His paly circlet, at his warning lamp
    The fragrant hours, and elves
    Who slept in buds the day,

And many a nymph who wreathes her brows with sedge,
And sheds the freshening dew, and, lovelier still,
    The pensive pleasures sweet,
    Prepare thy shadowy car:

Then lead, calm votaress, where some sheety lake
Cheers the lone heath, or some time-hallow'd pile,
    Or upland fallows grey
    Reflect its last cool gleam.

Or if chill blustering winds, or driving rain,
Prevent my willing feet, be mine the hut
    That from the mountain's side
    Views wilds and swelling floods,

And hamlets brown, and dim-discover'd spires,
And hears their simple bell, and marks o'er all
    Thy dewy fingers draw
    The gradual dusky veil.

While Spring shall pour his show'rs, as oft he wont,
And bathe thy breathing tresses, meekest Eve!
    While Summer loves to sport
    Beneath thy lingering light;

While sallow Autumn fills thy lap with leaves,
Or Winter, yelling through the troublous air,
    Affrights thy shrinking train,
    And rudely rends thy robes:

So long, regardful of thy quiet rule,
Shall Fancy, Friendship, Science, rose-lipp'd Health
    Thy gentlest influence own,
    And hymn thy favourite name!

WILLIAM COLLINS

Ode Written in 1746

How sleep the brave, who sink to rest
By all their country's wishes blest!
When Spring, with dewy fingers cold,
Returns·to deck their hallow'd mould,
She there shall dress a sweeter sod
Than Fancy's feet have ever trod.

By fairy hands their knell is rung;
By forms unseen their dirge is sung;
There Honour comes, a pilgrim grey,
To bless the turf that wraps their clay;
And Freedom shall awhile repair
To dwell, a weeping hermit, there!

WILLIAM COLLINS

The Village Scene

FROM *THE DESERTED VILLAGE*

Sweet Auburn! loveliest village of the plain,
Where health and plenty cheer'd the labouring swain,
Where smiling spring its earliest visit paid,
And parting summer's ling'ring blooms delayed:

Dear lovely bowers of innocence and ease,
Seats of my youth, when every sport could please,
How often have I loiter'd o'er thy green,
Where humble happiness endeared each scene;
How often have I paus'd on every charm,
The shelter'd cot, the cultivated farm,
The never-failing brook, the busy mill,
The decent church that topp'd the neighbouring hill,
The hawthorn bush, with seats beneath the shade,
For talking age and whisp'ring lovers made;
How often have I bless'd the coming day,
When toil remitting lent its turn to play,
And all the village train, from labour free,
Led up their sports beneath the spreading tree,
While many a pastime circled in the shade,
The young contending as the old survey'd;
And many a gambol frolick'd o'er the ground,
And sleights of art and feats of strength went round.
And still, as each repeated pleasure tir'd,
Succeeding sports the mirthful band inspir'd;
The dancing pair that simply sought renown
By holding out to tire each other down;
The swain mistrustless of his smutted face,
While secret laughter titter'd round the place;
The bashful virgin's side-long looks of love,
The matron's glance that would those looks reprove:
These were thy charms, sweet village; sports like these,
With sweet succession, taught even toil to please:
These round thy bowers their cheerful influence shed,
These were thy charms—but all these charms are fled.

Sweet smiling village, loveliest of the lawn,
Thy sports are fled, and all thy charms withdrawn;

Amidst thy bowers the tyrant's hand is seen,
And desolation saddens all the green:
One only master grasps the whole domain,
And half a tillage stints thy smiling plain.
No more thy glassy brook reflects the day,
But, chok'd with sedges, works its weedy way;
Along thy glades, a solitary guest,
The hollow-sounding bittern guards its nest;
Amidst thy desert walks the lapwing flies,
And tires their echoes with unvaried cries.

Sunk are thy bowers in shapeless ruin all,
And the long grass o'ertops the mould'ring wall;
And trembling, shrinking from the spoiler's hand,
Far, far away thy children leave the land.

Ill fares the land, to hast'ning ills a prey,
Where wealth accumulates, and men decay:
Princes and lords may flourish, or may fade;
A breath can make them, as a breath has made;
But a bold peasantry, their country's pride,
When once destroy'd, can never be supplied.

A time there was, ere England's grief began,
When every rood of ground maintain'd its man;
For him light labour spread her wholesome store,
Just gave what life requir'd, but gave no more:
His best companions, innocence and health;
And his best riches, ignorance of wealth.

But times are alter'd; trade's unfeeling train
Usurp the land and dispossess the swain;
Along the lawn, where scatter'd hamlets rose,

Unwieldy wealth and cumbrous pomp repose;
And every want to opulence allied,
And every pang that folly pays to pride.
Those gentle hours that plenty bade to bloom,
Those calm desires that ask'd but little room,
Those healthful sports that grac'd the peaceful scene,
Liv'd in each look, and brighten'd all the green;
These, far departing, seek a kinder shore,
And rural mirth and manners are no more.

OLIVER GOLDSMITH

Rural Sounds

FROM *THE TASK*

                  Mighty winds,
That sweep the skirt of some far-spreading wood
Of ancient growth, make music not unlike
The dash of ocean on his winding shore,
And lull the spirit while they fill the mind;
Unnumber'd branches waving in the blast,
And all their leaves fast flutt'ring, all at once.

Nor less composure waits upon the roar
Of distant floods, or on the softer voice
Of neighb'ring fountain, or of rills that slip
Through the cleft rock, and, chiming as they fall
Upon loose pebbles, lose themselves at length
In matted grass, that with a livelier green
Betrays the secret of their silent course.
Nature inanimate employs sweet sounds,
But animated nature sweeter still,
To soothe and satisfy the human ear.
Ten thousand warblers cheer the day, and one
The live-long night: nor these alone, whose notes
Nice finger'd art must emulate in vain,
But cawing rooks, and kites that swim sublime
In still repeated circles, screaming loud,
The jay, the pie, and ev'n the boding owl
That hails the rising moon, have charms for me.
Sounds inharmonious in themselves and harsh,
Yet heard in scenes where peace for ever reigns,
And only there, please highly for their sake.

WILLIAM COWPER

Where are the Swains?

FROM *THE VILLAGE*

Where are the swains, who, daily labour done,
With rural games play'd down the setting sun;
Who struck with matchless force the bounding ball,
Or made the pond'rous quoit obliquely fall;
While some huge Ajax, terrible and strong,

Engaged some artful stripling of the throng,
And fell beneath him, foil'd, while far around
Hoarse triumph rose, and rocks return'd the sound?
Where now are these?—Beneath yon cliff they stand,
To show the freighted pinnace where to land;
To load the ready steed with guilty haste,
To fly in terror o'er the pathless waste,
Or, when detected, in their straggling course,
To foil their foes by cunning or by force;
Or, yielding part (which equal knaves demand),
To gain a lawless passport through the land.
  Here, wand'ring long, amid these frowning fields,
I sought the simple life that Nature yields;
Rapine and Wrong and Fear usurp'd her place,
And a bold, artful, surly, savage race;
Who, only skill'd to take the finny tribe,
The yearly dinner, or septennial bribe,
Wait on the shore, and, as the waves run high,
On the tost vessel bend their eager eye,
Which to their coast directs its vent'rous way;
Theirs, or the ocean's, miserable prey.

GEORGE CRABBE

The Tyger

Tyger! Tyger! burning bright
In the forests of the night,
What immortal hand or eye
Could frame thy fearful symmetry?

In what distant deeps or skies
Burnt the fire of thine eyes?
On what wings dare he aspire?
What the hand dare seize the fire?

And what shoulder, and what art,
Could twist the sinews of thy heart?
And, when thy heart began to beat,
What dread hand? and what dread feet?

What the hammer? what the chain?
In what furnace was thy brain?
What the anvil? what dread grasp
Dare its deadly terrors clasp?

When the stars threw down their spears,
And watered heaven with their tears,
Did He smile His work to see?
Did He who made the Lamb make thee?

Tyger! Tyger! burning bright
In the forests of the night,
What immortal hand or eye,
Dare frame thy fearful symmetry?

WILLIAM BLAKE

The Clod and the Pebble

'Love seeketh not itself to please,
Nor for itself hath any care,
But for another gives its ease,
And builds a Heaven in Hell's despair.'

So sung a little Clod of Clay,
Trodden with the cattle's feet,
But a Pebble of the brook
Warbled out these metres meet:

'Love seeketh only self to please,
To bind another to its delight,
Joys in another's loss of ease,
And builds a Hell in Heaven's despite.'

WILLIAM BLAKE

Jerusalem

And did those feet in ancient time
    Walk upon England's mountains green?
And was the holy Lamb of God
    On England's pleasant pastures seen?

And did the Countenance Divine
  Shine forth upon our clouded hills?
And was Jerusalem builded here
  Among these dark Satanic mills?

Bring me my bow of burning gold!
  Bring me my arrows of desire!
Bring me my spear! O clouds, unfold!
  Bring me my chariot of fire!

I will not cease from mental fight,
  Nor shall my sword sleep in my hand,
Till we have built Jerusalem
  In England's green and pleasant land.

WILLIAM BLAKE

My Silks and Fine Array

My silks and fine array,
  My smiles and languish'd air,
By Love are driven away;
  And mournful lean Despair
Brings me yew to deck my grave;
Such end true lovers have.

His face is fair as heav'n
    When springing buds unfold:
O why to him was't giv'n,
    Whose heart is wintry cold?
His breast is love's all-worshipp'd tomb,
Where all love's pilgrims come.

Bring me an axe and spade,
    Bring me a winding-sheet;
When I my grave have made,
    Let winds and tempests beat:
Then down I'll lie as cold as clay:
True love doth pass away!

WILLIAM BLAKE

To the Evening Star

Thou fair-haired angel of the evening,
Now, while the sun rests on the mountains, light
Thy bright torch of love: thy radiant crown
Put on, and smile upon our evening bed!
Smile on our loves, and while thou drawest the
Blue curtains of the sky, scatter thy silver dew

On every flower that shuts its sweet eyes
In timely sleep. Let thy west wind sleep on
The lake; speak silence with thy glimmering eyes,
And wash the dusk with silver. Soon, full soon,
Dost thou withdraw; then the wolf rages wide,
And the lion glares through the dun forest:
The fleeces of our flocks are covered with
Thy sacred dew: protect them with thine influence.

WILLIAM BLAKE

My Bonnie Mary

Go fetch to me a pint o' wine,
   An' fill it in a silver tassie;
That I may drink before I go
   A service to my bonnie lassie:
The boat rocks at the pier o' Leith,
   Fu' loud the wind blaws frae the ferry,
The ship rides by the Berwick-law,
   And I maun leave my bonnie Mary.

The trumpets sound, the banners fly,
   The glittering spears are rankèd ready;
The shouts o' war are heard afar,
   The battle closes thick and bloody;
But it's no the roar o' sea or shore
   Wad make me langer wish to tarry;
Nor shout o' war that's heard afar—
   It's leaving thee, my bonnie Mary!

ROBERT BURNS

ROBERT BURNS

My Luve's like a Red, Red Rose

O, my Luve's like a red, red rose
  That's newly sprung in June:
O, my Luve's like the melodie
  That's sweetly played in tune!

As fair art thou, my bonnie lass,
  So deep in luve am I;
And I will luve thee still, my dear,
  Till a' the seas gang dry:

Till a' the seas gang dry, my dear,
  And the rocks melt wi' the sun;
I will luve thee still, my dear,
  While the sands o' life shall run.

And fare thee weel, my only Luve!
  And fare thee weel a while!
And I will come again, my Luve,
  Though it were ten thousand mile.

ROBERT BURNS

The Banks o' Doon

Ye flowery banks o' bonnie Doon,
  How can ye blume sae fair?
How can ye chant, ye little birds,
  And I sae fu' o' care?

Thou'll break my heart, thou bonnie bird,
  That sings upon the bough;
Thou minds me o' the happy days
  When my fause luve was true.

Thou'll break my heart, thou bonnie bird,
  That sings beside thy mate;
For sae I sat, and sae I sang,
  And wist na o' my fate.

Aft ha'e I roved by bonnie Doon,
  To see the wood-bine twine,
And ilka bird sang o' its love;
  And sae did I o' mine.

Wi' lightsome heart I pu'd a rose
  Frae off its thorny tree;
And my fause luver staw my rose,
  But left the thorn wi' me.

Wi' lightsome heart I pu'd a rose,
  Upon a morn in June;
And sae I flourish'd on the morn,
  And sae was pu'd ere noon.

ROBERT BURNS

The Solitary Reaper

Behold her, single in the field,
   Yon solitary Highland Lass!
Reaping and singing by herself;
   Stop here, or gently pass!
Alone she cuts and binds the grain,
And sings a melancholy strain:
O listen! for the Vale profound
Is overflowing with the sound.

No nightingale did ever chaunt
   More welcome notes to weary bands
Of travellers in some shady haunt,
   Among Arabian sands:
A voice so thrilling ne'er was heard
In spring-time from the Cuckoo-bird,
Breaking the silence of the seas
Among the farthest Hebrides.

Will no one tell me what she sings?—
   Perhaps the plaintive numbers flow
For old, unhappy, far-off things,
   And battles long ago:
Or is it some more humble lay.
Familiar matter of to-day?
Some natural sorrow, loss, or pain,
That has been, and may be again?

Whate'er the theme, the Maiden sang
   As if her song could have no ending;
I saw her singing at her work,

And o'er the sickle bending;—
I listened, motionless and still;
And, as I mounted up the hill,
The music in my heart I bore
Long after it was heard no more.

WILLIAM WORDSWORTH

Westminster Bridge

Earth has not anything to show more fair:
Dull would he be of soul who could pass by
A sight so touching in its majesty:
This City now doth, like a garment, wear
The beauty of the morning; silent, bare,
Ships, towers, domes, theatres, and temples lie
Open unto the fields, and to the sky;
All bright and glittering in the smokeless air.
Never did sun more beautifully steep
In his first splendour, valley, rock, or hill;
Ne'er saw I, never felt, a calm so deep!
The river glideth at his own sweet will:
Dear God! the very houses seem asleep;
And all that mighty heart is lying still!

WILLIAM WORDSWORTH

London, 1802

Milton! thou shouldst be living at this hour:
England hath need of thee: she is a fen
Of stagnant waters: altar, sword, and pen,
Fireside, the heroic wealth of hall and bower,
Have forfeited their ancient English dower
Of inward happiness. We are selfish men;
Oh! raise us up, return to us again;
And give us manners, virtue, freedom, power.
Thy soul was like a Star, and dwelt apart;
Thou hadst a voice whose sound was like the sea:
Pure as the naked heavens, majestic, free,
So didst thou travel on life's common way,
In cheerful godliness; and yet thy heart
The lowliest duties on herself did lay.

WILLIAM WORDSWORTH

An Ascent of Snowdon

FROM *THE PRELUDE*

It was a close, warm, breezeless summer night,
Wan, dull, and glaring, with a dripping fog
Low-hung and thick that covered all the sky;
But, undiscouraged, we began to climb

The mountain-side.   The mist soon girt us round,
And, after ordinary travellers' talk
With our conductor, pensively we sank
Each into commerce with his private thoughts:
Thus did we breast the ascent, and by myself
Was nothing either seen or heard that checked
Those musings or diverted, save that once
The shepherd's lurcher, who, among the crags,
Had to his joy unearthed a hedgehog, teased
His coiled-up prey with barkings turbulent.
This small adventure, for even such it seemed
In that wild place and at the dead of night,
Being over and forgotten, on we wound
In silence as before.   With forehead bent
Earthward, as if in opposition set
Against an enemy, I panted up
With eager pace, and no less eager thoughts.
Thus might we wear a midnight hour away,
Ascending at loose distance each from each,
And I, as chanced, the foremost of the band;
When at my feet the ground appeared to brighten,
And with a step or two seemed brighter still;
Nor was time given to ask or learn the cause,
For instantly a light upon the turf
Fell like a flash, and lo! as I looked up,
The Moon hung naked in a firmament
Of azure without cloud, and at my feet
Rested a silent sea of hoary mist.
A hundred hills their dusky backs upheaved
All over this still ocean; and beyond,
Far, far beyond, the solid vapours stretched,
In headlands, tongues, and promontory shapes,
Into the main Atlantic, that appeared

To dwindle, and give up his majesty,
Usurped upon far as the sight could reach.
Not so the ethereal vault; encroachment none
Was there, nor loss; only the inferior stars
Had disappeared, or shed a fainter light
In the clear presence of the full-orbed Moon,
Who, from her sovereign elevation, gazed
Upon the billowy ocean, as it lay
All meek and silent, save that through a rift—
Not distant from the shore whereon we stood,
A fixed, abysmal, gloomy, breathing-place—
Mounted the roar of waters, torrents, streams
Innumerable, roaring with one voice!
Heard over earth and sea, and, in that hour,
For so it seemed, felt by the starry heavens.
    When into air had partially dissolved
That vision, given to spirits of the night
And three chance human wanderers, in calm thought
Reflected, it appeared to me the type
Of a majestic intellect . . .

WILLIAM WORDSWORTH

The Daffodils

I wandered lonely as a cloud
That floats on high o'er vales and hills,
When all at once I saw a crowd,
A host, of golden daffodils;
Beside the lake, beneath the trees,
Fluttering and dancing in the breeze.

Continuous as the stars that shine
And twinkle on the milky way,
They stretched in never-ending line
Along the margin of a bay:
Ten thousand saw I at a glance,
Tossing their heads in sprightly dance.

The waves beside them danced, but they
Out-did the sparkling waves in glee:
A poet could not but be gay,
In such a jocund company:
I gazed—and gazed—but little thought
What wealth the show to me had brought:

For oft, when on my couch I lie
In vacant or in pensive mood,
They flash upon that inward eye
Which is the bliss of solitude;
  And then my heart with pleasure fills,
And dances with the daffodils.

WILLIAM WORDSWORTH

Proud Maisie

FROM *THE HEART OF MIDLOTHIAN*

Proud Maisie is in the wood,
  Walking so early;
Sweet Robin sits on the bush,
  Singing so rarely.

'Tell me, thou bonny bird,
  When shall I marry me?'
—'When six braw gentlemen
  Kirkward shall carry ye.'

'Who makes the bridal bed,
  Birdie, say truly?'
—'The grey-headed sexton
  That delves the grave duly.

'The glow-worm o'er grave and stone
  Shall light thee steady.
The owl from the steeple sing,
  Welcome, proud lady.'

SIR WALTER SCOTT

Lucy Ashton's Song

FROM *THE BRIDE OF LAMMERMOOR*

Look not thou on beauty's charming,
Sit thou still when kings are arming,
Taste not when the wine-cup glistens,
Speak not when the people listens,
Stop thine ear against the singer,
From the red gold keep thy finger,
Vacant heart and hand and eye,
Easy live and quiet die.

SIR WALTER SCOTT

Kubla Khan

In Xanadu did Kubla Khan
A stately pleasure-dome decree:
Where Alph, the sacred river, ran
Through caverns measureless to man
    Down to a sunless sea.
So twice five miles of fertile ground
With walls and towers were girdled round:
And there were gardens bright with sinuous rills,
Where blossomed many an incense-bearing tree:
And here were forests ancient as the hills,
    Enfolding sunny spots of greenery.
But oh! that deep romantic chasm which slanted
Down the green hill athwart a cedarn cover!
A savage place! as holy and enchanted

As e'er beneath a waning moon was haunted
By woman wailing for her demon-lover!
And from this chasm, with ceaseless turmoil seething,
As if this earth in fast thick pants were breathing,
A mighty fountain momently was forced:
Amid whose swift half-intermitted burst
Huge fragments vaulted like rebounding hail,
Or chaffy grain beneath the thresher's flail:
And mid these dancing rocks at once and ever
It flung up momently the sacred river.
Five miles meandering with a mazy motion
Through wood and dale the sacred river ran,
Then reached the caverns measureless to man,
And sank in tumult to a lifeless ocean:
And 'mid this tumult Kubla heard from far
Ancestral voices prophesying war!

  The shadow of the dome of pleasure
  Floated midway on the waves;
  Where was heard the mingled measure
  From the fountain and the caves.
It was a miracle of rare device,
A sunny pleasure-dome with caves of ice!

  A damsel with a dulcimer
  In a vision once I saw:
  It was an Abyssinian maid,
  And on her dulcimer she played,
  Singing of Mount Abora.
  Could I revive within me,
  Her symphony and song,
  To such a deep delight 'twould win me,
That with music loud and long,

I would build that dome in air,
That sunny dome! those caves of ice!
And all who heard should see them there,
And all should cry, Beware! Beware!
  His flashing eyes, his floating hair!
  Weave a circle round him thrice,
  And close your eyes with holy dread,
  For he on honey-dew hath fed,
  And drunk the milk of Paradise.

SAMUEL TAYLOR COLERIDGE

She walks in Beauty

She walks in beauty, like the night
  Of cloudless climes and starry skies;
And all that's best of dark and bright
  Meet in her aspect and her eyes:
Thus mellow'd to that tender light
  Which heaven to gaudy day denies.

One shade the more, one ray the less,
    Had half impair'd the nameless grace
Which waves in every raven tress,
    Or softly lightens o'er her face;
Where thoughts serenely sweet express
    How pure, how dear their dwelling-place.

And on that cheek, and o'er that brow,
    So soft, so calm, yet eloquent,
The smiles that win, the tints that glow,
    But tell of days in goodness spent,
A mind at peace with all below,
    A heart whose love is innocent!

LORD BYRON

The Coliseum

FROM *CHILDE HAROLD'S PILGRIMAGE*

But here, where Murder breathed her bloody steam;
And here, where buzzing nations choked the ways,
And roar'd or murmur'd like a mountain-stream
Dashing or winding as its torrent strays;
Here, where the Roman million's blame or praise
Was death or life, the playthings of a crowd,
My voice sounds much—and fall the stars' faint rays
On the arena void—seats crush'd,—walls bow'd—
And galleries, where my steps seem echoes strangely loud.

A ruin—yet what ruin! from its mass
Walls, palaces, half-cities, have been rear'd;
Yet oft the enormous skeleton ye pass,
And marvel where the spoil could have appear'd.
Hath it indeed been plunder'd, or but clear'd?
Alas! developed, opens the decay,
When the colossal fabric's form is near'd:
It will not bear the brightness of the day,
Which streams too much on all—years—man—have reft away.

But when the rising moon begins to climb
Its topmost arch, and gently pauses there;
When the stars twinkle through the loops of time,
And the low night-breeze waves along the air
The garland-forest, which the gray walls wear,
Like laurels on the bald first Cæsar's head;
When the light shines serene, but doth not glare,
Then in this magic circle raise the dead:
Heroes have trod this spot—'tis on their dust ye tread.

'While stands the Coliseum, Rome shall stand;
When falls the Coliseum, Rome shall fall;
And when Rome falls—the World.' From our own land
Thus spake the pilgrims o'er this mighty wall
In Saxon times, which we are wont to call
Ancient: and these three mortal things are still
On their foundations, and unalter'd all;
Rome and her Ruin past Redemption's skill,
The World, the same wide den—of thieves, or what ye will.

LORD BYRON

Music

Music, when soft voices die,
Vibrates in the memory—
Odours, when sweet violets sicken,
Live within the sense they quicken.
Rose leaves, when the rose is dead,
Are heaped for the belovèd's bed;
And so thy thoughts, when thou art gone,
Love itself shall slumber on.

PERCY BYSSHE SHELLEY

To a Skylark

Hail to thee, blithe Spirit!
Bird thou never wert,
That from Heaven, or near it,
Pourest thy full heart
In profuse strains of unpremeditated art.

Higher still and higher
From the earth thou springest
Like a cloud of fire;
The blue deep thou wingest,
And singing still dost soar, and soaring ever singest.

In the golden lightning
Of the sunken sun,
O'er which clouds are bright'ning
Thou dost float and run;
Like an unbodied joy whose race is just begun.

The pale purple even
Melts around thy flight;
Like a star of Heaven,
In the broad daylight
Thou art unseen, but yet I hear thy shrill delight,

Keen as are the arrows
Of that silver sphere,
Whose intense lamp narrows
In the white dawn clear
Until we hardly see—we feel that it is there.

All the earth and air
With thy voice is loud,
As, when night is bare,
From one lonely cloud
The moon rains out her beams, and Heaven is overflowed.

What thou art we know not;
What is most like thee?

From rainbow clouds there flow not
    Drops so bright to see
As from thy presence showers a rain of melody.

Like a Poet hidden
    In the light of thought,
Singing hymns unbidden,
    Till the world is wrought
To sympathy with hopes and fears it heeded not:

Like a high-born maiden
    In a palace-tower,
Soothing her love-laden
    Soul in secret hour
With music sweet as love, which overflows her bower:

Like a glow-worm golden
    In a dell of dew,
Scattering unbeholden
    Its aërial hue
Among the flowers and grass, which screen it from the view!

Like a rose embowered
    In its own green leaves,
By warm winds deflowered,
    Till the scent it gives
Makes faint with too much sweet those heavy-wingèd thieves:

Sound of vernal showers
    On the twinkling grass,
Rain-awakened flowers,
    All that ever was
Joyous, and clear, and fresh, thy music doth surpass:

Teach us, Sprite or Bird,
   What sweet thoughts are thine:
I have never heard
   Praise of love or wine
That panted forth a flood of rapture so divine.

Chorus Hymeneal
   Or triumphal chant,
Matched with thine, would be all
   But an empty vaunt,
A thing wherein we feel there is some hidden want.

What objects are the fountains
   Of thy happy strain?
What fields, or waves, or mountains?
   What shapes of sky or plain?
What love of thine own kind? what ignorance of pain?

With thy clear keen joyance
   Languor cannot be:
Shadow of annoyance
   Never came near thee:
Thou lovest—but ne'er knew love's sad satiety.

Waking or asleep
   Thou of death must deem
Things more true and deep
   Than we mortals dream,
Or how could thy notes flow in such a crystal stream?

We look before and after,
   And pine for what is not:

Our sincerest laughter
  With some pain is fraught;
Our sweetest songs are those that tell of saddest thought.

Yet if we could scorn
  Hate, and pride, and fear;
If we were things born
  Not to shed a tear,
I know not how thy joy we ever should come near.

Better than all measures
  Of delightful sound,
Better than all treasures
  That in books are found,
Thy skill to poet were, thou scorner of the ground!

Teach me half the gladness
  That thy brain must know,
Such harmonious madness
  From my lips would flow
The world should listen then—as I am listening now.

PERCY BYSSHE SHELLEY

Ode to the West Wind

I

O wild West Wind, thou breath of Autumn's being,
Thou, from whose unseen presence the leaves dead
Are driven, like ghosts from an enchanter fleeing,

Yellow, and black, and pale, and hectic red,
Pestilence-stricken multitudes—O thou
Who chariotest to their dark wintry bed

The wingèd seeds, where they lie cold and low,
Each like a corpse within its grave, until
Thine azure sister of the Spring shall blow

Her clarion o'er the dreaming earth, and fill
(Driving sweet buds like flocks to feed in air)
With living hues and odours plain and hill:

Wild Spirit, which art moving everywhere;
Destroyer and preserver; hear, oh, hear!

II

Thou on whose stream, mid the steep sky's commotion,
Loose clouds like earth's decaying leaves are shed,
Shook from the tangled boughs of Heaven and Ocean,

Angels of rain and lightning: there are spread
On the blue surface of thine aery surge,
Like the bright hair uplifted from the head

Of some fierce Mænad, even from the dim verge
Of the horizon to the zenith's height,
The locks of the approaching storm.   Thou dirge

Of the dying year, to which this closing night
Will be the dome of a vast sepulchre,
Vaulted with all thy congregated might

Of vapours, from whose solid atmosphere
Black rain, and fire, and hail will burst: oh, hear!

III

Thou who didst waken from his summer dreams
The blue Mediterranean, where he lay,
Lulled by the coil of his crystàlline streams,

Beside a pumice isle in Baiae's bay,
And saw in sleep old palaces and towers
Quivering within the wave's intenser day,

All overgrown with azure moss and flowers
So sweet, the sense faints picturing them! Thou
For whose path the Atlantic's level powers

Cleave themselves into chasms, while far below
The sea-blooms and the oozy woods which wear
The sapless foliage of the ocean, know

Thy voice and suddenly grow gray with fear,
And tremble and despoil themselves: oh, hear!

IV

If I were a dead leaf thou mightest bear;
If I were a swift cloud to fly with thee;
A wave to pant beneath thy power, and share

The impulse of thy strength, only less free
Than thou, O uncontrollable! If even
I were as in my boyhood, and could be

The comrade of thy wanderings over Heaven,
As then, when to outstrip thy skiey speed
Scarce seemed a vision; I would ne'er have striven

As thus with thee in prayer in my sore need.
Oh, lift me as a wave, a leaf, a cloud!
I fall upon the thorns of life! I bleed!

A heavy weight of hours has chained and bowed
One too like thee: tameless, and swift, and proud.

V

Make me thy lyre, even as the forest is:
What if my leaves are falling like its own!
The tumult of thy mighty harmonies

Will take from both a deep, autumnal tone,
Sweet though in sadness. Be thou, Spirit fierce,
My spirit! Be thou me, impetuous one!

Drive my dead thoughts over the universe
Like withered leaves to quicken a new birth!
And, by the incantation of this verse,

Scatter, as from an unextinguished hearth
Ashes and sparks, my words among mankind!
Be through my lips to unawakened earth

The trumpet of a prophecy! O, Wind,
If Winter comes, can Spring be far behind?

PERCY BYSSHE SHELLEY

Prometheus describes his Sufferings

FROM *PROMETHEUS UNBOUND*

The crawling glaciers pierce me with the spears
Of their moon-freezing crystals, the bright chains
Eat with their burning cold into my bones.
Heaven's wingèd hound, polluting from thy lips
His beak in poison not his own, tears up
My heart; and shapeless sights come wandering by,

The ghastly people of the realm of dream,
Mocking me: and the Earthquake-fiends are charged
To wrench the rivets from my quivering wounds
When the rocks split and close again behind:
While from their loud abysses howling throng
The genii of the storm, urging the rage
Of whirlwind, and afflict me with keen hail.

PERCY BYSSHE SHELLEY

I am

I am: yet what I am none cares or knows,
　My friends forsake me like a memory lost;
I am the self-consumer of my woes,
　They rise and vanish in oblivious host,
Like shades in love and death's oblivion lost;
And yet I am, and live with shadows tost

Into the nothingness of scorn and noise,
　Into the living sea of waking dreams,
Where there is neither sense of life nor joys,
　But the vast shipwreck of my life's esteems;
And e'en the dearest—that I loved the best—
Are strange—nay, rather stranger than the rest.

JOHN CLARE

I long for scenes where man has never trod,
    A place where woman never smiled or wept;
There to abide with my Creator, God,
    And sleep as I in childhood sweetly slept;
Untroubling and untroubled where I lie,
The grass below—above the vaulted sky.

JOHN CLARE

On first looking into Chapman's Homer

Much have I travell'd in the realms of gold,
    And many goodly states and kingdoms seen;
    Round many western islands have I been
Which bards in fealty to Apollo hold.
Oft of one wide expanse had I been told
    That deep-brow'd Homer rul'd as his demesne;
    Yet did I never breathe its pure serene
Till I heard Chapman speak out loud and bold:
Then felt I like some watcher of the skies
    When a new planet swims into his ken;
Or like stout Cortez, when with eagle eyes
    He star'd at the Pacific—and all his men
Look'd at each other with a wild surmise—
    Silent, upon a peak in Darien.

JOHN KEATS

To Autumn

Season of mists and mellow fruitfulness,
   Close bosom-friend of the maturing sun;
Conspiring with him how to load and bless
   With fruit the vines that round the thatch-eaves run;
To bend with apples the moss'd cottage-trees,
   And fill all fruit with ripeness to the core;
     To swell the gourd, and plump the hazel shells
   With a sweet kernel; to set budding more,
And still more, later flowers for the bees,
Until they think warm days will never cease,
     For Summer has o'er-brimm'd their clammy cells.

Who hath not seen thee oft amid thy store?
   Sometimes whoever seeks abroad may find
Thee sitting careless on a granary floor,
   Thy hair soft-lifted by the winnowing wind;
Or on a half-reap'd furrow sound asleep,
   Drowsed with the fume of poppies, while thy hook
     Spares the next swath and all its twinèd flowers;
And sometimes like a gleaner thou dost keep
   Steady thy laden head across a brook;
   Or by a cider-press, with patient look,
     Thou watchest the last oozings hours by hours.

Where are the songs of Spring? Ay, where are they?
   Think not of them, thou hast thy music too,
While barrèd clouds bloom the soft-dying day,
   And touch the stubble-plains with rosy hue;
Then in a wailful choir the small gnats mourn
   Among the river sallows, borne aloft

Or sinking as the light wind lives or dies;
And full-grown lambs loud bleat from hilly bourn;
Hedge-crickets sing; and now with treble soft
The red-breast whistles from a garden-croft;
And gathering swallows twitter in the skies.

JOHN KEATS

Ode on a Grecian Urn

I

Thou still unravish'd bride of quietness,
Thou foster-child of silence and slow time,
Sylvan historian, who canst thus express
A flowery tale more sweetly than our rhyme:
What leaf-fring'd legend haunts about thy shape
Of deities or mortals, or of both,
In Tempè or the dales of Arcady?
What men or gods are these? What maidens loth?
What mad pursuit? What struggle to escape?
What pipes and timbrels? What wild ecstasy?

II

Heard melodies are sweet, but those unheard
Are sweeter; therefore, ye soft pipes, play on;
Not to the sensual ear, but, more endear'd,
Pipe to the spirit ditties of no tone:

Fair youth, beneath the trees, thou canst not leave
  Thy song, nor ever can those trees be bare;
    Bold Lover, never, never canst thou kiss,
Though winning near the goal—yet, do not grieve;
  She cannot fade, though thou hast not thy bliss,
    For ever wilt thou love, and she be fair!

III

Ah, happy, happy boughs! that cannot shed
  Your leaves, nor ever bid the Spring adieu;
And, happy melodist, unwearièd,
  For ever piping songs for ever new;
More happy love! more happy, happy love!
  For ever warm and still to be enjoy'd,
    For ever panting, and for ever young;
All breathing human passion far above,
  That leaves a heart high-sorrowful and cloy'd,
    A burning forehead, and a parching tongue.

IV

Who are these coming to the sacrifice?
  To what green altar, O mysterious priest,
Lead'st thou that heifer lowing at the skies,
  And all her silken flanks with garlands drest?
What little town by river or sea shore,
  Or mountain-built with peaceful citadel,
    Is emptied of this folk, this pious morn?
And, little town, thy streets for evermore
  Will silent be; and not a soul to tell
    Why thou art desolate, can e'er return.

V

O Attic shape! Fair attitude! with brede
  Of marble men and maidens overwrought,
With forest branches and the trodden weed;
  Thou, silent form, dost tease us out of thought
As doth eternity: Cold Pastoral!
  When old age shall this generation waste,
    Thou shalt remain, in midst of other woe
Than ours, a friend to man, to whom thou say'st,
  'Beauty is truth, truth beauty,'—that is all
    Ye know on earth, and all ye need to know.

JOHN KEATS

Ode to a Nightingale

I

My heart aches, and a drowsy numbness pains
  My sense, as though of hemlock I had drunk,
Or emptied some dull opiate to the drains
  One minute past, and Lethe-wards had sunk:

Tis not through envy of thy happy lot,
  But being too happy in thine happiness,—
    That thou, light-wingèd Dryad of the trees,
      In some melodious plot
  Of beechen green, and shadows numberless,
    Singest of summer in full-throated ease.

II

O, for a draught of vintage! that hath been
  Cool'd a long age in the deep-delvèd earth,
Tasting of Flora and the country green,
  Dance, and Provençal song, and sunburnt mirth!
O for a beaker full of the warm South,
  Full of the true, the blushful Hippocrene,
    With beaded bubbles winking at the brim,
      And purple-stainèd mouth;
  That I might drink, and leave the world unseen,
    And with thee fade away into the forest dim:

III

Fade far away, dissolve, and quite forget
  What thou among the leaves hast never known,
The weariness, the fever, and the fret
  Here, where men sit and hear each other groan;
Where palsy shakes a few, sad, last gray hairs,
  Where youth grows pale, and spectre-thin, and dies;
    Where but to think is to be full of sorrow
      And leaden-eyed despairs;
  Where Beauty cannot keep her lustrous eyes,
    Or new Love pine at them beyond to-morrow.

IV

Away! away! for I will fly to thee,
  Not charioted by Bacchus and his pards,
But on the viewless wings of Poesy,
  Though the dull brain perplexes and retards:
Already with thee! tender is the night,
  And haply the Queen-Moon is on her throne,
    Cluster'd around by all her starry Fays;
      But here there is no light,
  Save what from heaven is with the breezes blown
    Through verdurous glooms and winding mossy ways.

V

I cannot see what flowers are at my feet,
  Nor what soft incense hangs upon the boughs,
But, in embalmèd darkness, guess each sweet
  Wherewith the seasonable month endows
The grass, the thicket, and the fruit-tree wild;
  White hawthorn, and the pastoral eglantine;
    Fast fading violets cover'd up in leaves;
      And mid-May's eldest child,
  The coming musk-rose, full of dewy wine,
    The murmurous haunt of flies on summer eves.

VI

Darkling I listen; and, for many a time
  I have been half in love with easeful Death,
Call'd him soft names in many a musèd rhyme,
  To take into the air my quiet breath;
Now more than ever seems it rich to die,

To cease upon the midnight with no pain,
   While thou art pouring forth thy soul abroad
      In such ecstasy!
Still wouldst thou sing, and I have ears in vain—
   To thy high requiem become a sod.

VII

Thou wast not born for death, immortal Bird!
   No hungry generations tread thee down;
The voice I hear this passing night was heard
   In ancient days by emperor and clown:
Perhaps the self-same song that found a path
   Through the sad heart of Ruth, when, sick for home,
     She stood in tears amid the alien corn;
       The same that oft-times hath
  Charm'd magic casements, opening on the foam
   Of perilous seas, in faery lands forlorn.

VIII

Forlorn! the very word is like a bell
   To toll me back from thee to my sole self!
Adieu! the fancy cannot cheat so well
   As she is fam'd to do, deceiving elf.
Adieu! adieu! thy plaintive anthem fades
   Past the near meadows, over the still stream,
     Up the hill-side; and now 'tis buried deep
      In the next valley-glades:
   Was it a vision, or a waking dream?
    Fled is that music :—Do I wake or sleep?

JOHN KEATS

A Thing of Beauty is a Joy for Ever

FROM *ENDYMION*

A thing of beauty is a joy for ever:
Its loveliness increases; it will never
Pass into nothingness; but still will keep
A bower quiet for us, and a sleep
Full of sweet dreams, and health, and quiet breathing.
Therefore, on every morrow, are we wreathing
A flowery band to bind us to the earth,
Spite of despondence, of the inhuman dearth
Of noble natures, of the gloomy days,
Of all the unhealthy and o'er-darkened ways
Made for our searching: yes, in spite of all,
Some shape of beauty moves away the pall
From our dark spirits. Such the sun, the moon,
Trees old, and young, sprouting a shady boon
For simple sheep; and such are daffodils
With the green world they live in; and clear rills
That for themselves a cooling covert make
'Gainst the hot season; the mid forest brake,
Rich with a sprinkling of fair musk-rose blooms:
And such too is the grandeur of the dooms
We have imagined for the mighty dead;
All lovely tales that we have heard or read:
An endless fountain of immortal drink,
Pouring unto us from the heaven's brink.

JOHN KEATS

La Belle Dame sans Merci

O what can ail thee, knight-at-arms,
  Alone and palely loitering?
The sedge is wither'd from the lake,
  And no birds sing.

O what can ail thee, knight-at-arms,
  So haggard and so woe-begone?
The squirrel's granary is full,
  And the harvest's done.

I see a lily on thy brow
  With anguish moist and fever dew;
And on thy cheek a fading rose
  Fast withereth too.

I met a lady in the meads
  Full beautiful—a faery's child,
Her hair was long, her foot was light,
  And her eyes were wild.

I made a garland for her head,
    And bracelets too, and fragrant zone;
She'd look'd at me as she did love,
    And made sweet moan.

I set her on my pacing steed,
    And nothing else saw all day long,
For sideways would she lean, and sing
    A faery's song.

She found me roots of relish sweet,
    And honey wild and manna dew,
And sure in language strange she said
    'I love thee true!'

She took me to her elfin grot,
    And there she wept and sigh'd full sore;
And there I shut her wild, wild eyes
    With kisses four.

And there she lullèd me asleep,
    And there I dream'd—Ah! woe betide!
The latest dream I ever dream'd
    On the cold hill's side.

I saw pale kings and princes too,
    Pale warriors, death-pale were they all:
Who cried—'La belle Dame sans Merci
    Hath thee in thrall!'

I saw their starved lips in the gloam
    With horrid warning gapèd wide,

And I awoke and found me here
  On the cold hill's side.

And this is why I sojourn here
  Alone and palely loitering,
Though the sedge is wither'd from the lake,
  And no birds sing.

JOHN KEATS

When I have Fears

When I have fears that I may cease to be
  Before my pen has glean'd my teeming brain,
Before high-pilèd books, in charactery,
  Hold like rich garners the full-ripen'd grain;
When I behold, upon the night's starr'd face,
  Huge cloudy symbols of a high romance,
And think that I may never live to trace
  Their shadows, with the magic hand of chance;
And when I feel, fair creature of an hour,
  That I shall never look upon thee more,
Never have relish in the faery power
  Of unreflecting love;—then on the shore
Of the wide world I stand alone, and think
Till love and fame to nothingness do sink.

JOHN KEATS

Time of Roses

It was not in the Winter
  Our loving lot was cast;
It was the time of roses—
  We pluck'd them as we pass'd!

That churlish season never frown'd
  On early lovers yet:
O no—the world was newly crown'd
  With flowers when first we met!

'Twas twilight, and I bade you go,
  But still you held me fast;
It was the time of roses—
  We pluck'd them as we pass'd.

THOMAS HOOD

Ruth

She stood breast high amid the corn,
Clasp'd by the golden light of morn,
Like the sweetheart of the sun,
Who many a glowing kiss had won.

On her cheek an autumn flush,
Deeply ripened;—such a blush
In the midst of brown was born,
Like red poppies grown with corn.

Round her eyes her tresses fell,
Which were blackest none could tell,
But long lashes veil'd a light
That had else been all too bright.

And her hat, with shady brim,
Made her tressy forehead dim;—
Thus she stood amid the stooks,
Praising God with sweetest looks:—

Sure, I said, Heav'n did not mean,
Where I reap thou shouldst but glean,
Lay thy sheaf adown and come,
Share my harvest and my home.

THOMAS HOOD

Ulysses

It little profits that an idle king,
By this still hearth, among these barren crags,
Match'd with an aged wife, I mete and dole
Unequal laws unto a savage race,
That hoard, and sleep, and feed, and know not me.
I cannot rest from travel: I will drink

Life to the lees: all times I have enjoy'd
Greatly, have suffer'd greatly, both with those
That loved me, and alone; on shore, and when
Thro' scudding drifts the rainy Hyades
Vext the dim sea: I am become a name;
For always roaming with a hungry heart
Much have I seen and known: cities of men
And manners, climates, councils, governments,
Myself not least, but honour'd of them all;
And drunk delight of battle with my peers,
Far on the ringing plains of windy Troy.
I am a part of all that I have met;
Yet all experience is an arch wherethro'
Gleams that untravell'd world, whose margin fades
For ever and for ever when I move.
How dull it is to pause, to make an end,
To rust unburnish'd, not to shine in use!
As tho' to breathe were life. Life piled on life
Were all too little, and of one to me
Little remains: but every hour is saved
From that eternal silence, something more,
A bringer of new things; and vile it were
For some three suns to store and hoard myself,
And this gray spirit yearning in desire
To follow knowledge, like a sinking star,
Beyond the utmost bound of human thought.
  This is my son, mine own Telemachus,
To whom I leave the sceptre and the isle—
Well-loved of me, discerning to fulfil
This labour, by slow prudence to make mild
A rugged people, and thro' soft degrees
Subdue them to the useful and the good.
Most blameless is he, centred in the sphere

Of common duties, decent not to fail
In offices of tenderness, and pay
Meet adoration to my household gods,
When I am gone. He works his work, I mine.
   There lies the port: the vessel puffs her sail:
There gloom the dark broad seas. My mariners,
Souls that have toil'd, and wrought, and thought with
     me—
That ever with a frolic welcome took
The thunder and the sunshine, and opposed
Free hearts, free foreheads—you and I are old;
Old age hath yet his honour and his toil;
Death closes all: but something ere the end,
Some work of noble note, may yet be done,
Not unbecoming men that strove with Gods.
The lights begin to twinkle from the rocks:
The long day wanes: the slow moon climbs: the deep
Moans round with many voices. Come, my friends,
'Tis not too late to seek a newer world.
Push off, and sitting well in order smite
The sounding furrows; for my purpose holds
To sail beyond the sunset, and the baths
Of all the western stars, until I die.
It may be that the gulfs will wash us down:
It may be we shall touch the Happy Isles,
And see the great Achilles, whom we knew.
Tho' much is taken, much abides; and tho'
We are not now that strength which in old days
Moved earth and heaven; that which we are, we are;
One equal temper of heroic hearts,
Made weak by time and fate, but strong in will
To strive, to seek, to find, and not to yield.

LORD TENNYSON

LORD TENNYSON

The Lady of Shalott

PART I

On either side the river lie
Long fields of barley and of rye,
That clothe the wold and meet the sky;
And thro' the field the road runs by
   To many-tower'd Camelot;
And up and down the people go,
Gazing where the lilies blow
Round an island there below,
   The island of Shalott.

Willows whiten, aspens quiver,
Little breezes dusk and shiver
Thro' the wave that runs for ever
By the island in the river
   Flowing down to Camelot.
Four grey walls, and four grey towers,
Overlook a space of flowers,
And the silent isle imbowers
   The Lady of Shalott.

By the margin, willow-veil'd,
Slide the heavy barges trail'd
By slow horses; and unhail'd
The shallop flitteth silken-sail'd
        Skimming down to Camelot:
But who hath seen her wave her hand?
Or at 'the casement seen her stand?
Or is she known in all the land,
        The Lady of Shalott?

Only reapers, reaping early
In among the bearded barley,
Hear a song that echoes cheerly
From the river winding clearly,
        Down to tower'd Camelot:
And by the moon the reaper weary,
Piling sheaves in uplands airy,
Listening, whispers ''Tis the fairy
        Lady of Shalott.'

PART II

There she weaves by night and day
A magic web with colours gay.
She has heard a whisper say,
A curse is on her if she stay
        To look down to Camelot.
She knows not what the curse may be,
And so she weaveth steadily,
And little other care hath she,
        The Lady of Shalott.

And moving thro' a mirror clear
That hangs before her all the year,
Shadows of the world appear.
There she sees the highway near
        Winding down to Camelot:
There the river eddy whirls,
And there the surly village-churls,
And the red cloaks of market girls,
        Pass onward from Shalott.

Sometimes a troop of damsels glad,
An abbot on an ambling pad,
Sometimes a curly shepherd-lad,
Or long-hair'd page in crimson clad
        Goes by to tower'd Camelot;
And sometimes thro' the mirror blue
The knights come riding two and two:
She hath no loyal knight and true,
        The Lady of Shalott.

But in her web she still delights
To weave the mirror's magic sights,
For often thro' the silent nights
A funeral, with plumes and lights
        And music, went to Camelot:
Or when the moon was overhead,
Came two young lovers lately wed;
'I am half sick of shadows,' said
        The Lady of Shalott.

PART III

A bow-shot from her bower-eaves,
He rode between the barley-sheaves,
The sun came dazzling thro' the leaves,
And flamed upon the brazen greaves
   Of bold Sir Lancelot.
A red-cross knight for ever kneel'd
To a lady in his shield,
That sparkled on the yellow field,
   Beside remote Shalott.

The gemmy bridle glitter'd free,
Like to some branch of stars we see
Hung in the golden Galaxy.
The bridle bells rang merrily
   As he rode down to Camelot:
And from his blazon'd baldric slung
A mighty silver bugle hung,
And as he rode his armour rung,
   Beside remote Shalott.

All in the blue unclouded weather
Thick-jewell'd shone the saddle leather,
The helmet and the helmet-feather
Burn'd like one burning flame together,
   As he rode down to Camelot.
As often thro' the purple night,
Below the starry clusters bright,
Some bearded meteor, trailing light,
   Moves over still Shalott.

His broad clear brow in sunlight glow'd;
On burnish'd hooves his war-horse trode;
From underneath his helmet flow'd
His coal-black curls as on he rode,
      As he rode down to Camelot.
From the bank and from the river
He flash'd into the crystal mirror,
'Tirra lirra,' by the river
      Sang Sir Lancelot.

She left the web, she left the loom,
She made three paces thro' the room,
She saw the water-lily bloom,
She saw the helmet and the plume,
      She look'd down to Camelot.
Out flew the web and floated wide;
The mirror crack'd from side to side;
'The curse is come upon me,' cried
      The Lady of Shalott.

PART IV

In the stormy east-wind straining,
The pale yellow woods were waning,
The broad stream in his banks complaining,
Heavily the low sky raining
      Over tower'd Camelot;
Down she came and found a boat
Beneath a willow left afloat,
And round about the prow she wrote
      The Lady of Shalott.

And down the river's dim expanse—
Like some bold seër in a trance,
Seeing all his own mischance—
With a glassy countenance
        Did she look to Camelot.
And at the closing of the day
She loosed the chain, and down she lay;
The broad stream bore her far away,
        The Lady of Shalott.

Lying, robed in snowy white
That loosely flew to left and right—
The leaves upon her falling light—
Thro' the noises of the night
        She floated down to Camelot:
And as the boat-head wound along
The willowy hills and fields among,
They heard her singing her last song,
        The Lady of Shalott.

Heard a carol, mournful, holy,
Chanted loudly, chanted lowly,
Till her blood was frozen slowly,
And her eyes were darken'd wholly,
        Turn'd to tower'd Camelot;
For ere she reach'd upon the tide
The first house by the water-side,
Singing in her song she died,
        The Lady of Shalott.

Under tower and balcony,
By garden-wall and gallery,

A gleaming shape she floated by,
Dead-pale between the houses high,
      Silent into Camelot.
Out upon the wharfs they came,
Knight and burgher, lord and dame,
And round the prow they read her name,
      The Lady of Shalott.

Who is this? and what is here?
And in the lighted palace near
Died the sound of royal cheer;
And they cross'd themselves for fear,
      All the knights at Camelot:
But Lancelot mused a little space;
He said, 'She has a lovely face;
God in His mercy lend her grace,
      The Lady of Shalott.'

LORD TENNYSON

Home-Thoughts, from Abroad

Oh, to be in England
Now that April's there,
And whoever wakes in England
Sees, some morning, unaware,
That the lowest boughs and the brushwood sheaf
Round the elm-tree bole are in tiny leaf,
While the chaffinch sings on the orchard bough
In England—now!

And after April, when May follows,
And the whitethroat builds, and all the swallows!
Hark! where my blossomed pear-tree in the hedge
Leans to the field and scatters on the clover
Blossoms and dewdrops—at the bent spray's edge—
That's the wise thrush; he sings each song twice over,
Lest you should think he never could recapture
The first fine careless rapture!
And though the fields look rough with hoary dew,
All will be gay when noontide wakes anew
The buttercups, the little children's dower
—Far brighter than this gaudy melon-flower!

ROBERT BROWNING

Prospice

Fear death?—to feel the fog in my throat,
 The mist in my face,
When the snows begin, and the blasts denote
 I am nearing the place,
The power of the night, the press of the storm,
 The post of the foe;
Where he stands, the Arch Fear in a visible form,
 Yet the strong man must go:
For the journey is done and the summit attained,
 And the barriers fall,
Though a battle's to fight ere the guerdon be gained,
 The reward of it all.

I was ever a fighter, so—one fight more,
    The best and the last!
I would hate that death bandaged my eyes, and forbore,
    And bade me creep past.
No! let me taste the whole of it, fare like my peers
    The heroes of old,
Bear the brunt, in a minute pay glad life's arrears
    Of pain, darkness and cold.
For sudden the worst turns the best to the brave,
    The black minute's at end,
And the elements' rage, the fiend-voices that rave,
    Shall dwindle, shall blend,
Shall change, shall become first a peace, then a joy
    Then a light, then thy breast,
O thou soul of my soul! I shall clasp thee again,
    And with God be the rest!

ROBERT BROWNING

'Childe Roland to the Dark Tower came'

(*See Edgar's Song in* Lear)

I

My first thought was, he lied in every word,
    That hoary cripple, with malicious eye
    Askance to watch the working of his lie
On mine, and mouth scarce able to afford
Suppression of the glee that pursed and scored
    Its edge at one more victim gained thereby.

II

What else should he be set for, with his staff?
   What, save to waylay with his lies, ensnare
   All travellers that might find him posted there,
And ask the road? I guessed what skull-like laugh
Would break, what crutch 'gin write my epitaph
   For pastime' in the dusty thoroughfare,

III

If at his counsel I should turn aside
   Into that ominous tract which, all agree,
   Hides the Dark Tower.   Yet acquiescingly
I did turn as he pointed; neither pride
Nor hope rekindling at the end descried,
   So much as gladness that some end might be.

IV

For, what with my whole world-wide wandering,
   What with my search drawn out thro' years, my hope
   Dwindled into a ghost not fit to cope
With that obstreperous joy success would bring,—
I hardly tried now to rebuke the spring
   My heart made, finding failure in its scope.

V

As when a sick man very near to death
   Seems dead indeed, and feels begin and end
   The tears and takes the farewell of each friend,
And hears one bid the other go, draw breath

Freelier outside, ('since all is o'er,' he saith,
'And the blow fallen no grieving can amend');

VI

While some discuss if near the other graves
Be room enough for this, and when a day
Suits best for carrying the corpse away,
With care about the banners, scarves and staves,—
And still the man hears all, and only craves
He may not shame such tender love and stay.

VII

Thus, I had so long suffered in this quest,
Heard failure prophesied so oft, been writ
So many times among 'The Band!'—to wit,
The knights who to the Dark Tower's search addressed
Their steps—that just to fail as they, seemed best.
And all the doubt was now—should I be fit?

VIII

So, quiet as despair, I turned from him,
That hateful cripple, out of his highway
Into the path he pointed. All the day
Had been a dreary one at best, and dim
Was settling to its close, yet shot one grim
Red leer to see the plain catch its estray.

IX

For mark! no sooner was I fairly found
Pledged to the plain, after a pace or two,

Than, pausing to throw backward a last view
To the safe road, 'twas gone; grey plain all round:
Nothing but plain to the horizon's bound.
    I might go on; nought else remained to do.

X

So, on I went. I think I never saw
    Such starved ignoble nature; nothing throve:
    For flowers—as well expect a cedar grove!
But cockle, spurge, according to their law
Might propagate their kind, with none to awe,
    You'd think; a burr had been a treasure-trove.

XI

No! penury, inertness and grimace,
    In some strange sort, were the land's portion. 'See
    Or shut your eyes,' said Nature peevishly,
'It nothing skills: I cannot help my case:
'Tis the last Judgement's fire must cure this place,
    Calcine its clods and set my prisoners free.'

XII

If there pushed any ragged thistle-stalk
    Above its mates, the head was chopped—the bents
    Were jealous else. What made those holes and rents
In the dock's harsh swarth leaves—bruised as to baulk
All hope of greenness? 'tis a brute must walk
    Pashing their life out, with a brute's intents.

XIII

As for the grass, it grew as scant as hair
  In leprosy; thin dry blades pricked the mud
  Which underneath looked kneaded up with blood.
One stiff blind horse, his every bone a-stare,
Stood stupefied, however he came there:
  Thrust out past service from the devil's stud!

XIV

Alive? he might be dead for aught I know,
  With that red, gaunt and colloped neck a-strain,
  And shut eyes underneath the rusty mane;
Seldom went such grotesqueness with such woe;
I never saw a brute I hated so;
  He must be wicked to deserve such pain.

XV

I shut my eyes and turned them on my heart.
  As a man calls for wine before he fights,
  I asked one draught of earlier, happier sights,
Ere fitly I could hope to play my part.
Think first, fight afterwards—the soldier's art:
  One taste of the old time sets all to rights!

XVI

Not it! I fancied Cuthbert's reddening face
  Beneath its garniture of curly gold,
  Dear fellow, till I almost felt him fold
An arm in mine to fix me to the place,

That way he used. Alas! one night's disgrace!
  Out went my heart's new fire and left it cold.

XVII

Giles, then, the soul of honour—there he stands
  Frank as ten years ago when knighted first.
  What honest men should dare (he said) he durst.
Good—but the scene shifts—faugh! what hangman's hands
Pin to his breast a parchment? his own bands
  Read it. Poor traitor, spit upon and curst!

XVIII

Better this Present than a Past like that;
  Back therefore to my darkening path again.
  No sound, no sight as far as eye could strain.
Will the night send a howlet or a bat?
I asked: when something on the dismal flat
  Came to arrest my thoughts and change their train.

XIX

A sudden little river crossed my path
  As unexpected as a serpent comes.
  No sluggish tide congenial to the glooms—
This, as it frothed by, might have been a bath
For the fiend's glowing hoof—to see the wrath
  Of its black eddy bespate with flakes and spumes.

XX

So petty yet so spiteful! all along,
  Low scrubby alders kneeled down over it;

Drenched willows flung them headlong in a fit
Of mute despair, a suicidal throng:
The river which had done them all the wrong,
   Whate'er that was, rolled by, deterred no whit.

XXI

Which, while I forded,—good saints, how I feared
   To set my foot upon a dead man's cheek,
   Each step, or feel the spear I thrust to seek
For hollows, tangled in his hair or beard!
—It may have been a water-rat I speared,
   But, ugh! it sounded like a baby's shriek.

XXII

Glad was I when I reached the other bank.
   Now for a better country.   Vain presage!
   Who were the strugglers, what war did they wage,
Whose savage trample thus could pad the dank
Soil to a plash? toads in a poisoned tank,
   Or wild cats in a red-hot iron cage—

XXIII

The fight must so have seemed in that fell cirque.
   What penned them there, with all the plain to choose?
   No footprint leading to that horrid mews,
None out of it.   Mad brewage set to work
Their brains, no doubt, like galley-slaves the Turk
   Pits for his pastime, Christians against Jews.

XXIV

And more than that—a furlong on—why, there!
  What bad use was that engine for, that wheel,
  Or brake, not wheel—that harrow fit to reel
Men's bodies out like silk? with all the air
Of Tophet's tool, on earth left unaware,
  Or brought to sharpen its rusty teeth of steel.

XXV

Then came a bit of stubbed ground, once a wood,
  Next a marsh, it would seem, and now mere earth
  Desperate and done with; (so a fool finds mirth,
Makes a thing and then mars it, till his mood
Changes and off he goes!) within a rood—
  Bog, clay and rubble, sand and stark black dearth.

XXVI

Now blotches rankling, coloured gay and grim,
  Now patches where some leanness of the soil's
  Broke into moss or substances like boils;
Then came some palsied oak, a cleft in him
Like a distorted mouth that splits its rim
  Gaping at death, and dies while it recoils.

XXVII

And just as far as ever from the end!
  Nought in the distance but the evening, nought
  To point my footsteps further! At the thought,
A great black bird, Apollyon's bosom-friend,

Sailed past, nor beat his wide wing dragon-penned
   That brushed my cap—perchance the guide I sought.

XXVIII

For, looking up, aware I somehow grew,
   'Spite of the dusk the plain had given place
   All round to mountains—with such name to grace
Mere ugly heights and heaps now stolen in view.
How thus they had surprised me,—solve it, you!
   How to get from them was no clearer case.

XXIX

Yet half I seemed to recognize some trick
   Of mischief happened to me, God knows when—
   In a bad dream perhaps. Here ended, then,
Progress this way. When, in the very nick
Of giving up, one time more, came a click
   As when a trap shuts—you're inside the den!

XXX

Burningly it came on me all at once,
   This was the place! those two hills on the right,
   Crouched like two bulls locked horn in horn in fight;
While to the left, a tall scalped mountain . . . Dunce,
Fool, to be dozing at the very nonce,
   After a life spent training for the sight!

XXXI

What in the midst lay but the Tower itself?
   The round squat turret, blind as the fool's heart,

Built of brown stone, without a counterpart
In the whole world. The tempest's mocking elf
Points to the shipman thus the unseen shelf
   He strikes on, only when the timbers start.

XXXII

Not see? because of night perhaps?—Why, day
   Came back again for that! before it left,
   The dying sunset kindled through a cleft:
The hills, like giants at a hunting, lay,
Chin upon hand, to see the game at bay,—
   'Now stab and end the creature—to the heft!'

XXXIII

Not hear? when noise was everywhere! it tolled
   Increasing like a bell. Names in my ears,
   Of all the lost adventurers my peers,—
How such a one was strong, and such was bold,
And such was fortunate, yet each of old
   Lost, lost! one moment knelled the woe of years.

XXXIV

There they stood, ranged along the hillsides, met
   To view the last of me, a living frame
   For one more picture! in a sheet of flame
I saw them and I knew them all. And yet
Dauntless the slug-horn to my lips I set,
   And blew. '*Childe Roland to the Dark Tower came.*'

ROBERT BROWNING

My Last Duchess

FERRARA

That's my last Duchess painted on the wall,
Looking as if she were alive. I call
That piece a wonder, now : Frà Pandolf's hands
Worked busily a day, and there she stands.
Will't please you sit and look at her ? I said
'Frà Pandolf' by design, for never read
Strangers like you that pictured countenance,
The depth and passion of its earnest glance,
But to myself they turned (since none puts by
The curtain I have drawn for you, but I)
And seemed as they would ask me, if they durst,
How such a glance came there , so, not the first
Are you to turn and ask thus. Sir, 'twas not
Her husband's presence only, called that spot
Of joy into the Duchess' cheek : perhaps
Frà Pandolf chanced to say 'Her mantle laps
Over my Lady's wrist too much,' or 'Paint
Must never hope to reproduce the faint
Half-flush that dies along her throat' : such stuff
Was courtesy, she thought, and cause enough
For calling up that spot of joy. She had
A heart—how shall I say ?—too soon made glad,
Too easily impressed ; she liked whate'er
She looked on, and her looks went everywhere
Sir, 'twas all one ! My favour at her breast,
The dropping of the daylight in the West,
The bough of cherries some officious fool
Broke in the orchard for her, the white mule
She rode with round the terrace—all and each

Would draw from her alike the approving speech,
Or blush, at least. She thanked men,—good! but thanked
Somehow—I know not how—as if she ranked
My gift of a nine-hundred-years-old name
With anybody's gift. Who'd stoop to blame
This sort of trifling? Even had you skill
In speech—(which I have not)—to make your will
Quite clear to such an one, and say, 'Just this
Or that in you disgusts me; here you miss,
Or there exceed the mark'—and if she let
Herself be lessoned so, nor plainly set
Her wits to yours, forsooth, and made excuse,
—E'en then would be some stooping; and I choose
Never to stoop. Oh sir, she smiled, no doubt,
Whene'er I passed her; but who passed without
Much the same smile? This grew; I gave commands;
Then all smiles stopped together. There she stands
As if alive. Will't please you rise? We'll meet
The company below, then. I repeat,
The Count your master's known munificence
Is ample warrant that no just pretence
Of mine for dowry will be disallowed;
Though his fair daughter's self, as I avowed
At starting, is my object. Nay, we'll go
Together down, sir. Notice Neptune, though,
Taming a sea-horse, thought a rarity,
Which Claus of Innsbruck cast in bronze for me!

ROBERT BROWNING

Shakespeare

Others abide our question.   Thou art free.
We ask and ask: Thou smilest and art still,
Out-topping knowledge.   For the loftiest hill
That to the stars uncrowns his majesty,
Planting his steadfast footsteps in the sea,
Making the heaven of heavens his dwelling-place,
Spares but the cloudy border of his base
To the foil'd searching of mortality:
And thou, who didst the stars and sunbeams know,
Self-school'd, self-scann'd, self-honour'd, self-secure,
Didst walk on earth unguess'd at.   Better so!
All pains the immortal spirit must endure,
  All weakness that impairs, all griefs that bow,
  Find their sole voice in that victorious brow.

MATTHEW ARNOLD

Dover Beach

The sea is calm to-night.
The tide is full, the moon lies fair
Upon the straits; on the French coast the light
Gleams, and is gone; the cliffs of England stand,
Glimmering and vast, out in the tranquil bay.
Come to the window, sweet is the night air!
Only, from the long line of spray
Where the sea meets the moon-blanch'd land,
Listen! you hear the grating roar

Of pebbles which the waves draw back, and fling,
At their return, up the high strand,
Begin, and cease, and then again begin,
With tremulous cadence slow, and bring
The eternal note of sadness in.

Sophocles long ago
Heard it on the Ægean, and it brought
Into his mind the turbid ebb and flow
Of human misery; we
Find also in the sound a thought,
Hearing it by this distant northern sea.

The Sea of Faith
Was once, too, at the full, and round earth's shore
Lay like the folds of a bright girdle furl'd.
But now I only hear
Its melancholy, long, withdrawing roar,
Retreating, to the breath
Of the night-wind, down the vast edges drear
And naked shingles of the world.

Ah, love, let us be true
To one another! for the world, which seems
To lie before us like a land of dreams,
So various, so beautiful, so new,
Hath really neither joy, nor love, nor light,
Nor certitude, nor peace, nor help for pain;
And we are here as on a darkling plain
Swept with confused alarms of struggle and flight
Where ignorant armies clash by night.

MATTHEW ARNOLD

The Scholar Gypsy

Go, for they call you, Shepherd, from the hill ;
  Go, Shepherd, and untie the wattled cotes :
    No longer leave thy wistful flock unfed,
  Nor let thy bawling fellows rack their throats,
    Nor the cropp'd grasses shoot another head.
      But when the fields are still,
  And the tired men and dogs all gone to rest,
    And only the white sheep are sometimes seen
    Cross and recross the strips of moon-blanch'd green,
  Come, Shepherd, and again begin the quest.

Here, where the reaper was at work of late,
  In this high field's dark corner, where he leaves
    His coat, his basket, and his earthen cruse,
  And in the sun all morning binds the sheaves,
    Then here, at noon, comes back his stores to use ;
      Here will I sit and wait,
  While to my ear from uplands far away
    The bleating of the folded flocks is borne,
    With distant cries of reapers in the corn—
  All the live murmur of a summer's day.

Screen'd is this nook o'er the high, half-reap'd field,
  And here till sun-down, Shepherd, will I be.
    Through the thick corn the scarlet poppies peep,
  And round green roots and yellowing stalks I see
    Pale blue convolvulus in tendrils creep ;
      And air-swept lindens yield
  Their scent, and rustle down their perfum'd showers
    Of bloom on the bent grass where I am laid,
    And bower me from the August sun with shade ;
  And the eye travels down to Oxford's towers :

And near me on the grass lies Glanvil's book—
  Come, let me read the oft-read tale again,
    The story of that Oxford scholar poor
  Of pregnant parts and quick inventive brain,
    Who, tir'd of knocking at Preferment's door,
      One summer morn forsook
  His friends, and went to learn the Gypsy lore,
    And roam'd the world with that wild brotherhood,
    And came, as most men deem'd, to little good,
  But came to Oxford and his friends no more.

But once, years after, in the country lanes,
  Two scholars whom at college erst he knew
    Met him, and of his way of life enquir'd.
  Whereat he answer'd, that the Gypsy crew,
    His mates, had arts to rule as they desir'd
      The workings of men's brains ;
  And they can bind them to what thoughts they will :
    'And I,' he said, 'the secret of their art,
    When fully learn'd, will to the world impart :
  But it needs heaven-sent moments for this skill.'

This said, he left them, and return'd no more,
    But rumours hung about the countryside
        That the lost Scholar long was seen to stray,
    Seen by rare glimpses, pensive and tongue-tied,
        In hat of antique shape, and cloak of grey,
            The same the Gypsies wore.
    Shepherds had met him on the Hurst in spring ;
        At some lone alehouse in the Berkshire moors,
        On the warm ingle bench, the smock-frock'd boors
    Had found him seated at their entering,

But, mid their drink and clatter, he would fly :
    And I myself seem half to know thy looks,
        And put the shepherds, Wanderer, on thy trace ;
    And boys who in lone wheatfields scare the rooks
        I ask if thou hast pass'd their quiet place ;
            Or in my boat I lie
    Moor'd to the cool bank in the summer heats,
        Mid wide grass meadows which the sunshine fills,
        And watch the warm green-muffled Cumner hills,
    And wonder if thou haunt'st their shy retreats.

For most, I know, thou lov'st retirèd ground.
    Thee, at the ferry, Oxford riders blithe,
        Returning home on summer nights, have met
    Crossing the stripling Thames at Bab-lock-hithe,
        Trailing in the cool stream thy fingers wet,
            As the slow punt swings round :
    And leaning backwards in a pensive dream,
        And fostering in thy lap a heap of flowers
        Pluck'd in shy fields and distant Wychwood bowers,
    And thine eyes resting on the moonlit stream.

And then they land, and thou art seen no more.
   Maidens who from the distant hamlets come
     To dance around the Fyfield elm in May,
   Oft through the darkening fields have seen thee roam,
     Or cross a stile into the public way.
       Oft thou hast given them store
   Of flowers—the frail-leaf'd, white anemone—
     Dark bluebells drench'd with dews of summer eves—
     And purple orchises with spotted leaves—
   But none has words she can report of thee.

And, above Godstow Bridge, when hay-time's here
   In June, and many a scythe in sunshine flames,
     Men who through those wide fields of breezy grass
   Where black-wing'd swallows haunt the glittering Thames,
     To bathe in the abandon'd lasher pass,
       Have often pass'd thee near
   Sitting upon the river bank o'ergrown :
     Mark'd thy outlandish garb, thy figure spare,
     Thy dark vague eyes, and soft abstracted air ;
   But, when they came from bathing, thou wert gone.

At some lone homestead in the Cumner hills,
   Where at her open door the housewife darns,
     Thou hast been seen, or hanging on a gate
   To watch the threshers in the mossy barns.
     Children, who early range these slopes and late
       For cresses from the rills,
   Have known thee watching, all an April day,
     The springing pastures and the feeding kine ;
     And mark'd thee, when the stars come out and shine,
   Through the long dewy grass move slow away.

In autumn, on the skirts of Bagley Wood,
  Where most the gypsies by the turf-edg'd way
    Pitch their smok'd tents, and every bush you see
With scarlet patches tagg'd and shreds of grey,
    Above the forest ground call'd Thessaly—
      The blackbird picking food
Sees thee, nor stops his meal, nor fears at all ;
    So often has he known thee past him stray
    Rapt, twirling in thy hand a wither'd spray,
And waiting for the spark from Heaven to fall.

And once, in winter, on the causeway chill
  Where home through flooded fields foot-travellers go,
    Have I not pass'd thee on the wooden bridge
Wrapt in thy cloak and battling with the snow,
    Thy face towards Hinksey and its wintry ridge ?
      And thou hast climb'd the hill
And gain'd the white brow of the Cumner range,
    Turn'd once to watch, while thick the snowflakes fall,
    The line of festal light in Christ-Church hall—
Then sought thy straw in some sequester'd grange.

But what—I dream ! Two hundred years are flown
  Since first thy story ran through Oxford halls,
    And the grave Glanvil did the tale inscribe
That thou wert wander'd from the studious walls
    To learn strange arts, and join a Gypsy-tribe :
      And thou from earth art gone
Long since, and in some quiet churchyard laid—
    Some country nook, where o'er thy unknown grave
    Tall grasses and white flowering nettles wave—
Under a dark red-fruited yew-tree's shade.

—No, no, thou hast not felt the lapse of hours.
  For what wears out the life of mortal men ?
    'Tis that from change to change their being rolls :
  'Tis that repeated shocks, again, again,
    Exhaust the energy of strongest souls,
      And numb the elastic powers.
  Till having us'd our nerves with bliss and teen,
    And tir'd upon a thousand schemes our wit,
    To the just-pausing Genius we remit
  Our worn-out life, and are—what we have been.

Thou hast not liv'd, why should'st thou perish, so ?
  Thou hadst *one* aim, *one* business, *one* desire :
    Else wert thou long since number'd with the dead !
  Else hadst thou spent, like other men, thy fire !
    The generations of thy peers are fled,
      And we ourselves shall go ;
  But thou possessest an immortal lot,
    And we imagine thee exempt from age
    And living as thou liv'st on Glanvil's page,
  Because thou hadst—what we, alas, have not !

For early didst thou leave the world, with powers
  Fresh, undiverted to the world without,
    Firm to their mark, not spent on other things ;
  Free from the sick fatigue, the languid doubt,
    Which much to have tried, in much been baffled, brings
      O life unlike to ours !
  Who fluctuate idly without term or scope,
    Of whom each strives, nor knows for what he strives,
    And each half lives a hundred different lives ;
  Who wait like thee, but not, like thee, in hope.

Thou waitest for the spark from Heaven : and we,
   Vague half-believers of our casual creeds,
     Who never deeply felt, nor clearly will'd,
   Whose insight never has borne fruit in deeds,
     Whose weak resolves never have been fulfill'd ;
       For whom each year we see
   Breeds new beginnings, disappointments new ;
     Who hesitate and falter life away,
     And lose to-morrow the ground won to-day—
Ah, do not we, Wanderer, await it too ?

Yes, we await it, but it still delays,
   And then we suffer ; and amongst us One,
     Who most has suffer'd, takes dejectedly
   His seat upon the intellectual throne ;
     And all his store of sad experience he
       Lays bare of wretched days ;
   Tells us his misery's birth and growth and signs,
     And how the dying spark of hope was fed,
     And how the breast was sooth'd, and how the head,
And all his hourly varied anodynes.

This for our wisest : and we others pine,
   And wish the long unhappy dream would end,
     And waive all claim to bliss, and try to bear
   With close-lipp'd Patience for our only friend,
     Sad Patience, too near neighbour to Despair :
       But none has hope like thine.
   Thou through the fields and through the woods dost stray,
     Roaming the countryside, a truant boy,
     Nursing thy project in unclouded joy,
And every doubt long blown by time away.

O born in days when wits were fresh and clear,
  And life ran gaily as the sparkling Thames ;
    Before this strange disease of modern life,
  With its sick hurry, it divided aims,
    Its heads o'ertax'd, its palsied hearts, was rife—
      Fly hence, our contact fear !
Still fly, plunge deeper in the bowering wood !
  Averse, as Dido did with gesture stern
  From her false friend's approach in Hades turn,
Wave us away, and keep thy solitude.

Still nursing the unconquerable hope,
  Still clutching the inviolable shade,
    With a free onward impulse brushing through,
  By night, the silver'd branches of the glade—
    Far on the forest skirts, where none pursue,
      On some mild pastoral slope
Emerge, and resting on the moonlit pales,
  Freshen thy flowers, as in former years,
  With dew, or listen with enchanted ears,
From the dark dingles, to the nightingales.

But fly our paths, our feverish contact fly !
  For strong the infection of our mental strife,
    Which, though it gives no bliss, yet spoils for rest ;
  And we should win thee from thy own fair life,
    Like us distracted, and like us unblest.
      Soon, soon thy cheer would die,
Thy hopes grow timorous, and unfix'd thy powers,
  And thy clear aims be cross and shifting made :
  And then thy glad perennial youth would fade,
Fade, and grow old at last, and die like ours.

Then fly our greetings, fly our speech and smiles !
   —As some grave Tyrian trader, from the sea,
     Descried at sunrise an emerging prow
  Lifting the cool-haired creepers stealthily,
     The fringes of a southward-facing brow
       Among the Aegean isles :
  And saw the merry Grecian coaster come,
     Freighted with amber grapes, and Chian wine,
     Green bursting figs, and tunnies steep'd in brine ;
  And knew the intruders on his ancient home,

The young light-hearted Masters of the waves ;
     And snatch'd his rudder, and shook out more sail,
     And day and night held on indignantly
  O'er the blue Midland waters with the gale,
     Betwixt the Syrtes and soft Sicily
       To where the Atlantic raves
  Outside the Western Straits, and unbent sails
     There, where down cloudy cliffs, through sheets of foam,
     Shy traffickers, the dark Iberians come ;
  And on the beach undid his corded bales.

MATTHEW ARNOLD

vague half-believers = *light* in the editions of 1853–54
weak resolves = *vague* in the editions of 1853–54

Battle-Hymn of the Republic

Mine eyes have seen the glory of the coming of the Lord:
He is trampling out the vintage where the grapes of wrath
  are stored;

He hath loosed the fateful lightning of his terrible swift
    sword.
        His truth is marching on.

I have seen Him in the watch-fires of a hundred circling
    camps;
They have builded Him an altar in the evening dews and
    damps;
I can read His righteous sentence by the dim and flaring
    lamps.
        His day is marching on.

I have read a fiery gospel, writ in burnished rows of steel:
'As ye deal with my contemners, so with you my grace
    shall deal;
Let the Hero, born of woman, crush the serpent with his
    heel,
        Since God is marching on.'

He has sounded forth the trumpet that shall never call
    retreat;
He is sifting out the hearts of men before his judgment-seat;
Oh! be swift, my soul, to answer Him! be jubilant, my
    feet!
        Our God is marching on.

In the beauty of the lilies Christ was born across the sea,
With a glory in his bosom that transfigures you and me:
As He died to make men holy, let us die to make men free,
        While God is marching on.

                    JULIA WARD HOWE

The Train

I like to see it lap the miles,
And lick the valleys up,
And stop to feed itself at tanks;
And then, prodigious, step

Around a pile of mountains,
And, supercilious, peer
In shanties by the sides of roads;
And then a quarry pare

To fit its sides, and crawl between,
Complaining all the while
In horrid, hooting stanza;
Then chase itself down hill

And neigh like Boanerges;
Then, punctual as a star,
Stop—docile and omnipotent—
At its own stable door.

EMILY DICKINSON

PART TWO

In Time of 'The Breaking of Nations'

Only a man harrowing clods
  In a slow silent walk
With an old horse that stumbles and nods
  Half asleep as they stalk.

Only thin smoke without flame
  From the heaps of couch-grass;
Yet this will go onward the same
  Though Dynasties pass.

Yonder a maid and her wight
  Come whispering by;
War's annals will cloud into night
  Ere their story die.

THOMAS HARDY

In the British Museum

What do you see in that time-touched stone,
  When nothing is there
But ashen blankness, although you give it
  A rigid stare?

'You look not quite as if you saw,
    But as if you heard,
Parting your lips, and treading softly
    As mouse or bird.

'It is only the base of a pillar, they'll tell you,
    That came to us
From a far old hill men used to name
    Areopagus.'

—'I know no art, and I only view
    A stone from a wall,
But I am thinking that stone has echoed
    The voice of Paul,

'Paul as he stood and preached beside it
    Facing the crowd,
A small gaunt figure with wasted features,
    Calling out loud

'Words that in all their intimate accents
    Pattered upon
That marble front, and were wide reflected,
    And then were gone.

'I'm a labouring man, and know but little,
    Or nothing at all;
But I can't help thinking that stone once echoed
    The voice of Paul.'

                THOMAS HARDY

On a Midsummer Eve

I idly cut a parsley stalk
And blew therein towards the moon;
I had not thought what ghosts would walk
With shivering footsteps to my tune.

I went, and knelt, and scooped my hand
As if to drink, into the brook,
And a faint figure seemed to stand
Above me, with the bygone look.

I lipped rough rhymes of chance, not choice,
I thought not what my words might be;
There came into my ear a voice
That turned a tenderer verse for me.

THOMAS HARDY

God's Grandeur

The world is charged with the grandeur of God.
   It will flame out, like shining from shook foil;
   It gathers to a greatness, like the ooze of oil
Crushed. Why do men then now not reck his rod?
Generations have trod, have trod, have trod;
   And all is seared with trade; bleared, smeared with toil;
   And wears man's smudge and shares man's smell: the soil
Is bare now, nor can foot feel, being shod.
And for all this, nature is never spent;

There lives the dearest freshness deep down things;
And though the last lights off the black West went
  Oh, morning, at the brown brink eastward, springs—
Because the Holy Ghost over the bent
  World broods with warm breast and with ah! bright
    wings.

GERARD MANLEY HOPKINS

As Kingfishers catch fire

As kingfishers catch fire, dragonflies dràw flàme;
As tumbled over rim in roundy wells
Stones ring; like each tucked string tells, each hung bell's
Bow swung finds tongue to fling out broad its name;
Each mortal thing does one thing and the same:
Deals out that being indoors each one dwells;
Selves—goes itself; *myself* it speaks and spells,
Crying *Whàt I do is me: for that I came.*

I say mòre: the just man justices;
Kèeps gràce: thàt keeps all his goings graces;
Acts in God's eye what in God's eye he is—
Chrìst—for Christ plays in ten thousand places,
Lovely in limbs, and lovely in eyes not his
To the Father through the features of men's faces.

GERARD MANLEY HOPKINS

Pied Beauty

Glory be to God for dappled things—
   For skies of couple-colour as a brinded cow;
     For rose-moles all in stipple upon trout that swim;
Fresh-firecoal chestnut-falls; finches' wings;
   Landscape plotted and pieced—fold, fallow, and plough;
     And àll tràdes, their gear and tackle and trim.

All things counter, original, spare, strange;
   Whatever is fickle, freckled (who knows how?)
     With swift, slow; sweet, sour; adazzle, dim;
He fathers-forth whose beauty is past change:
         Praise him.

GERARD MANLEY HOPKINS

Spring

Nothing is so beautiful as spring—
   When weeds, in wheels, shoot long and lovely and lush;
   Thrush's eggs look little low heavens, and thrush
Through the echoing timber does so rinse and wring
The ear, it strikes like lightnings to hear him sing;

The glassy pear-tree leaves and blooms, they brush
  The descending blue; that blue is all in a rush
With richness; the racing lambs too have fair their fling.

What is all this juice and all this joy?
  A strain of the earth's sweet being in the beginning
In Eden garden.—Have, get, before it cloy,
  Before it cloud, Christ, lord, and sour with sinning,
Innocent mind and Mayday in girl and boy,
  Most, O maid's child, thy choice and worthy the winning.

GERARD MANLEY HOPKINS

The Starlight Night

Look at the stars! look, look up at the skies!
  O look at all the fire-folk sitting in the air!
  The bright boroughs, the circle-citadels there!
Down in dim woods the diamond delves! the elves'-eyes!
The grey lawns cold where gold, where quickgold lies!
  Wind-beat whitebeam! airy abeles set on a flare!
  Flake-doves sent floating forth at a farmyard scare!—
Ah well! it is all a purchase, all is a prize.

Buy then! bid then!—What?—Prayer, patience, alms, vows.
Look, look: a May-mess, like on orchard boughs!
  Look! March-bloom, like on mealed-with-yellow sallows!

These are indeed the barn; withindoors house
The shocks. This piece-bright paling shuts the spouse
  Christ home, Christ and his mother and all his hallows.

GERARD MANLEY HOPKINS

Nightingales

Beautiful must be the mountains whence ye come,
  And bright in the fruitful valleys the streams, wherefrom
      Ye learn your song:
Where are those starry woods? O might I wander there,
  Among the flowers, which in that heavenly air
      Bloom the year long!

Nay, barren are those mountains and spent the streams:
  Our song is the voice of desire, that haunts our dreams,
      A throe of the heart,
Whose pining visions dim, forbidden hopes profound,
  No dying cadence nor long sigh can sound,
      For all our art.

Alone, aloud in the raptured ear of men
  We pour our dark nocturnal secret; and then,
      As night is withdrawn
From these sweet-springing meads and bursting boughs of
  May,
  Dream, while the innumerable choir of day
      Welcome the dawn.

ROBERT BRIDGES

A Passer-by

Whither, O splendid ship, thy white sails crowding,
  Leaning across the bosom of the urgent West,
That fearest nor sea rising, nor sky clouding,
  Whither away, fair rover, and what thy quest?
  Ah! soon, when Winter has all our vales opprest,
When skies are cold and misty, and hail is hurling,
  Wilt thóu glíde on the blue Pacific, or rest
In a summer haven asleep, thy white sails furling.

I there before thee, in the country that well thou knowest,
  Already arrived am inhaling the odorous air:
I watch thee enter unerringly where thou goest,
  And anchor queen of the strange shipping there,
  Thy sails for awnings spread, thy masts bare;
Nor is aught from the foaming reef to the snow-capped,
    grandest
  Peak, that is over the feathery palms, more fair
Than thou, so upright, so stately, and still thou standest.

And yet, O splendid ship, unhailed and nameless,
  I know not if, aiming a fancy, I rightly divine
That thou hast a purpose joyful, a courage blameless,
  Thy port assured in a happier land than mine.
  But for all I have given thee, beauty enough is thine,
As thou, aslant with trim tackle and shrouding,
  From the proud nostril curve of a prow's line
In the offing scatterest foam, thy white sails crowding.

ROBERT BRIDGES

To a Snowflake

What heart could have thought you?—
Past our devisal
(O filigree petal!)
Fashioned so purely,
Fragilely, surely,
From what Paradisal
Imagineless metal,
Too costly for cost?
Who hammered you, wrought you,
From argentine vapour?—
'God was my shaper.
Passing surmisal,
He hammered, He wrought me,
From curled silver vapour,
To lust of His mind:—
Thou couldst not have thought me!
So purely, so palely,
Tinily, surely,
Mightily, frailly,
Insculped and embossed,
With His hammer of wind,
And His graver of frost.'

FRANCIS THOMPSON

The Kingdom of God

'In No Strange Land'

O world invisible, we view thee,
  O world intangible, we touch thee,
O world unknowable, we know thee,
  Inapprehensible, we clutch thee!

Does the fish soar to find the ocean,
  The eagle plunge to find the air—
That we ask of the stars in motion
  If they have rumour of thee there?

Not where the wheeling systems darken,
  And our benumbed conceiving soars!—
The drift of pinions, would we hearken,
  Beats at our own clay-shuttered doors.

The angels keep their ancient places;—
  Turn but a stone, and start a wing!
'Tis ye, 'tis your estrangèd faces,
  That miss the many-splendoured thing.

FRANCIS THOMPSON

But (when so sad thou canst not sadder)
   Cry;—and úpon thy so sore loss
Shall shine the traffic of Jacob's ladder
   Pitched betwixt Heaven and Charing Cross.

Yea, in the night, my Soul, my daughter,
   Cry,—clinging Heaven by the hems;
And lo, Christ walking on the water
   Not of Gennesareth, but Thames!

FRANCIS THOMPSON

Bredon Hill

In summertime on Bredon
   The bells they sound so clear;
Round both the shires they ring them
   In steeples far and near,
   A happy noise to hear.

Here of a Sunday morning
   My love and I would lie,
And see the coloured counties,
   And hear the larks so high
   About us in the sky.

The bells would ring to call her
   In valleys miles away:
'Come all to church, good people;
   Good people, come and pray.'
   But here my love would stay.

ALFRED EDWARD HOUSMAN

And I would turn and answer
  Among the springing thyme,
'Oh, peal upon our wedding,
  And we will hear the chime,
  And come to church in time.'

But when the snows at Christmas
  On Bredon top were strown,
My love rose up so early
  And stole out unbeknown
  And went to church alone.

They tolled the one bell only,
  Groom there was none to see,
The mourners followed after,
  And so to church went she,
  And would not wait for me.

The bells they sound on Bredon,
  And still the steeples hum.
'Come all to church, good people,'—
  Oh, noisy bells, be dumb;
  I hear you, I will come.

ALFRED EDWARD HOUSMAN

Loveliest of Trees

Loveliest of trees, the cherry now
Is hung with bloom along the bough,
And stands about the woodland ride
Wearing white for Eastertide.

Now, of my threescore years and ten,
Twenty will not come again,
And take from seventy springs a score,
It only leaves me fifty more.

And since to look at things in bloom
Fifty springs are little room,
About the woodlands I will go
To see the cherry hung with snow.

ALFRED EDWARD HOUSMAN

When summer's end is nighing

When summer's end is nighing
And skies at evening cloud,
I muse on change and fortune
And all the feats I vowed
When I was young and proud.

The weathercock at sunset
Would lose the slanted ray,
And I would climb the beacon

That looked to Wales away
And saw the last of day.

From hill and cloud and heaven
  The hues of evening died;
Night welled through lane and hollow
  And hushed the countryside,
  But I had youth and pride.

And I with earth and nightfall
  In converse high would stand,
Late, till the west was ashen
  And darkness hard at hand,
  And the eye lost the land.

The year might age, and cloudy
  The lessening day might close,
But air of other summers
  Breathed from beyond the snows,
  And I had hope of those.

They came and were and are not
  And come no more anew;
And all the years and seasons
  That ever can ensue
  Must now be worse and few.

So here's an end of roaming
  On eves when autumn nighs:
The ear too fondly listens
  For summer's parting sighs,
  And then the heart replies.

ALFRED EDWARD HOUSMAN

Written on Dew

Dew drenched the heath all silver grey
And glimmering white at peep of day;
Each thorn and blade a treasure bears
Won of the sad dawn mother's tears,
Where Eos wept her Memnon slain
Again, again.

Over the dew there runs a blur
To tell some early wanderer:
The passing of field-mouse's paws,
The patter of a plover's claws,
Or other little child of time
Upon the rime.

The shadowy trail is gone apace;
Its trivial message leaves no trace,
But fades for none again to find
At touch of risen sun and wind.
Conscious, unconscious—there are few
Even mark the dew.

EDEN PHILLPOTTS

An Irish Airman foresees his Death

I know that I shall meet my fate
Somewhere among the clouds above;
Those that I fight I do not hate,
Those that I guard I do not love;

My country is Kiltartan Cross,
My countrymen Kiltartan's poor,
No likely end could bring them loss
Or leave them happier than before.
Nor law, nor duty bade me fight,
Nor public men, nor cheering crowds,
A lonely impulse of delight
Drove to this tumult in the clouds;
I balanced all, brought all to mind,
The years to come seemed waste of breath,
A waste of breath the years behind
In balance with this life, this death.

WILLIAM BUTLER YEATS

Aedh wishes for the Cloths of Heaven

Had I the heavens' embroidered cloths,
    Enwrought with golden and silver light,
The blue and the dim and the dark cloths
    Of night and light and the half light,
  would spread the cloths under your feet:
    But I, being poor, have only my dreams;
I have spread my dreams under your feet;
    Tread softly because you tread on my dreams.

WILLIAM BUTLER YEATS

The Wild Swans at Coole

The trees are in their autumn beauty,
The woodland paths are dry,
Under the October twilight the water
Mirrors a still sky;
Upon the brimming water among the stones
Are nine-and-fifty swans.

The nineteenth Autumn has come upon me
Since I first made my count;
I saw, before I had well finished,
All suddenly mount
And scatter wheeling in great broken rings
Upon their clamorous wings.

I have looked upon those brilliant creatures,
And now my heart is sore.
All's changed since I, hearing at twilight,
The first time on this shore,
The bell-beat of their wings above my head,
Trod with a lighter tread.

Unwearied still, lover by lover,
They paddle in the cold
Companionable streams or climb the air;
Their hearts have not grown old;
Passion or conquest, wander where they will,
Attend upon them still.

But now they drift on the still water,
Mysterious, beautiful;
Among what rushes will they build,
By what lake's edge or pool
Delight men's eyes when I awake some day
To find they have flown away?

WILLIAM BUTLER YEATS

Sailing to Byzantium

That is no country for old men. The young
In one another's arms, birds in the trees,
—Those dying generations—at their song,
The salmon-falls, the mackerel-crowded seas,
Fish, flesh, or fowl, commend all summer long
Whatever is begotten, born, and dies.
Caught in that sensual music all neglect
Monuments of unageing intellect.

An aged man is but a paltry thing,
A tattered coat upon a stick, unless
Soul clap its hands and sing, and louder sing
For every tatter in its mortal dress,
Nor is there singing school but studying
Monuments of its own magnificence;
And therefore I have sailed the seas and come
To the holy city of Byzantium.

O sages standing in God's holy fire
As in the gold mosaic of a wall,
Come from the holy fire, perne in a gyre,
And be the singing-masters of my soul.
Consume my heart away; sick with desire
And fastened to a dying animal
It knows not what it is; and gather me
Into the artifice of eternity.

Once out of nature I shall never take
My bodily form from any natural thing,
But such a form as Grecian goldsmiths make
Of hammered gold and gold enamelling
To keep a drowsy Emperor awake;
Or set upon a golden bough to sing
To lords and ladies of Byzantium
Of what is past, or passing, or to come.

WILLIAM BUTLER YEATS

When you are old

When you are old and grey and full of sleep,
And nodding by the fire, take down this book,
And slowly read, and dream of the soft look
Your eyes had once, and of their shadows deep;

How many loved your moments of glad grace,
And loved your beauty with love false or true;
But one man loved the pilgrim soul in you,
And loved the sorrows of your changing face.

And bending down beside the glowing bars,
Murmur, a little sadly, how Love fled
And paced upon the mountains overhead
And hid his face amid a crowd of stars.

WILLIAM BUTLER YEATS

Cities and Thrones and Powers

Cities and Thrones and Powers,
   Stand in Time's eye,
Almost as long as flowers,
   Which daily die:
But, as new buds put forth
   To glad new men,
Out of the spent and unconsidered Earth,
   The Cities rise again.

This season's Daffodil,
    She never hears
What change, what chance, what chill,
    Cut down last year's;
But with bold countenance,
    And knowledge small,
Esteems her seven days' continuance,
    To be perpetual.

So Time that is o'er-kind
    To all that be,
Ordains us e'en as blind,
    As bold as she:
That in our very death,
    And burial sure,
Shadow to shadow, well persuaded, saith,
    'See how our works endure!'

RUDYARD KIPLING

Cuckoo!

In woods so long time bare
  Cuckoo!
Up and in the wood, I know not where
Two notes fall.
Yet I do not envy him at all
His phantasy.
Cuckoo!
I too,
Somewhere,
I have sung as merrily as he
Who can dare,
Small and careless lover, so to laugh at care,
And who
Can call
Cuckoo!
In woods of winter weary,
In scented woods, of winter weary, call
Cuckoo!
In woods so long time bare.

HILAIRE BELLOC

Ha'nacker Mill

Sally is gone that was so kindly
    Sally is gone from Ha'nacker Hill.
And the Briar grows ever since then so blindly
    And ever since then the clapper is still,
    And the sweeps have fallen from Ha'nacker Mill.

Ha'nacker Hill is in Desolation:
    Ruin a-top and a field unploughed.
And Spirits that call on a falling nation
    Spirits that loved her calling aloud:
    Spirits abroad in a windy cloud.

Spirits that call and no one answers;
    Ha'nacker's down and England's done.
Wind and Thistle for pipe and dancers
    And never a ploughman under the Sun.
    Never a ploughman.   Never a one.

                        HILAIRE BELLOC

The Song of Honour

I climbed a hill as light fell short,
And rooks came home in scramble sort,
And filled the trees and flapped and fought
And sang themselves to sleep;
An owl from nowhere with no sound
Swung by and soon was nowhere found,

I heard him calling half-way round,
Holloing loud and deep;
A pair of stars, faint pins of light,
Then many a star, sailed into sight,
And all the stars, the flower of night,
Were round me at a leap;
To tell how still the valleys lay
I heard a watchdog miles away,
And bells of distant sheep.

I heard no more of bird or bell,
The mastiff in a slumber fell,
I stared into the sky,
As wondering men have always done
Since beauty and the stars were one,
Though none so hard as I.

It seemed, so still the valleys were,
As if the whole world knelt at prayer,
Save me and me alone;
So pure and wide that silence was
I feared to bend a blade of grass,
And there I stood like stone.
There, sharp and sudden, there I heard—

Ah! some wild lovesick singing bird
Woke singing in the trees?
The nightingale and babble-wren
Were in the English greenwood then,
And you heard one of these?

The babble-wren and nightingale
Sang in the Abysinnian vale
That season of the year!
Yet, true enough, I heard them plain,
I heard them both again, again,
As sharp and sweet and clear
As if the Abyssinian tree
Had thrust a bough across the sea,
Had thrust a bough across to me
With music for my ear!

I heard them both, and oh! I heard
The song of every singing bird
That sings beneath the sky,
And with the song of lark and wren
The song of mountains, moths and men
And seas and rainbows vie!

I heard the universal choir,
The Sons of Light exalt their Sire
With universal song,
Earth's lowliest and loudest notes,
Her million times ten million throats
Exalt Him loud and long,
And lips and lungs and tongues of Grace
From every part and every place
Within the shining of His face,
The universal throng.

I heard the hymn of being sound
From every well of honour found
In human sense and soul

The song of poets when they write
The testament of Beautysprite
Upon a flying scroll,
The song of painters when they take
A burning brush for Beauty's sake
And limn her features whole—

The song of men divinely wise
Who look and see in starry skies
Not stars so much as robins' eyes,
And when these pale away
Hear flocks of shiny pleiades
Among the plums and apple trees
Sing in the summer day—

The song of all both high and low
To some blest vision true,
The song of beggars when they throw
The crust of pity all men owe
To hungry sparrows in the snow,
Old beggars hungry too—
The song of kings of kingdoms when
They rise above their fortune Men,
And crown themselves anew—

The song of courage, heart and will
And gladness in a fight,
Of men who face a hopeless hill
With sparking and delight,
The bells and bells of song that ring
Round banners of a cause or king
From armies bleeding white—

The song of sailors every one
When monstrous tide and tempest run
At ships like bulls at red,
When stately ships are twirled and spun
Like whipping tops and help there's none
And mighty ships ten thousand ton
Go down like lumps of lead—

And song of fighters stern as they
At odds with fortune night and day,
Crammed up in cities grim and grey
As thick as bees in hives,
Hosannas of a lowly throng
Who sing unconscious of their song,
Whose lips are in their lives—

And song of some at holy war
With spells and ghouls more dread by far
Than deadly seas and cities are
Or hordes of quarrelling kings—
The song of fighters great and small.
The song of pretty fighters all
And high heroic things—

The song of lovers—who knows how
Twitched up from place and time
Upon a sigh, a blush, a vow,
A curve or hue of cheek or brow,
Borne up and off from here and now
Into the void sublime!

15

And crying loves and passions still
In every key from soft to shrill
And numbers never done,
Dog-loyalties to faith and friend,
And loves like Ruth's of old no end,
And intermission none—

And burst on burst for beauty and
For numbers not behind,
From men whose love of motherland
Is like a dog's for one dear hand,
Sole, selfless, boundless, blind—
And song of some with hearts beside
For men and sorrows far and wide,
Who watch the world with pity and pride
And warm to all mankind—

And endless joyous music rise
From children at their play,
And endless soaring lullabies
From happy, happy mothers' eyes,
And answering crows and baby-cries,
How many who shall say!
And many a song as wondrous well
With pangs and sweets intolerable

From lonely hearths too grey to tell,
God knows how utter grey!
And song from many a house of care
When pain has forced a footing there
And there's a Darkness on the stair
Will not be turned away—

And song—that song whose singers come
With old kind tales of pity from
The Great Compassion's lips,
That make the bells of Heaven to peal
Round pillows frosty with the feel
Of Death's cold finger tips—

The song of men all sorts and kinds,
As many tempers, moods and minds
As leaves are on a tree,
As many faiths and castes and creeds,
As many human bloods and breeds
As in the world may be;
The song of each and all who gaze
On Beauty in her naked blaze,
Or see her dimly in a haze,
Or get her light in fitful rays
And tiniest needles even,
The song of all not wholly dark,
Not wholly sunk in stupor stark
Too deep for groping Heaven—

And alleluias sweet and clear
And wild with beauty men mishear,
From choirs of song as near and dear
To Paradise as they,
The everlasting pipe and flute
Of wind and sea and bird and brute,
And lips deaf men imagine mute
In wood and stone and clay:

The music of a lion strong
That shakes a hill a whole night long,
A hill as loud as he,
The twitter of a mouse among
Melodious greenery,
The ruby's and the rainbow's song,
The nightingale's—all three,
The song of life that wells and flows
From every leopard, lark and rose
And everything that gleams or goes
Lack-lustre in the sea.

I heard it all, each, every note
Of every lung and tongue and throat,
Ay, every rhythm and rhyme
Of everything that lives and loves
And upward, ever upward moves
From lowly to sublime!
Earth's multitudinous Sons of Light,
I heard them lift their lyric might
With each and every chanting sprite
That lit the sky that wondrous night
As far as eye could climb!

I heard it all, I heard the whole
Harmonious hymn of being roll
Up through the chapel of my soul
And at the altar die,
And in the awful quiet then
Myself I heard Amen, Amen,
Amen I heard me cry!
I heard it all and then although

I caught my flying senses, Oh,
A dizzy man was I!
I stood and stared; the sky was lit,
The sky was stars all over it,
I stood, I knew not why,
Without a wish, without a will,
I stood upon that silent hill
And stared into the sky until
My eyes were blind with stars and still
I stared into the sky.

RALPH HODGSON

The Scribe

What lovely things
Thy hand hath made:
The smooth-plumed bird
In its emerald shade,
The seed of the grass,
The speck of stone
Which the wayfaring ant
Stirs—and hastes on!
Though I should sit

By some tarn in thy hills,
Using its ink
As the spirit wills
To write of Earth's wonders,
Its live, willed things,
Flit would the ages
On soundless wings
Ere unto Z
My pen drew nigh;
Leviathan told,
And the honey-fly:
And still would remain
My wit to try—
My worn reeds broken
The dark tarn dry,
All words forgotten—
Thou, Lord, and I.

WALTER DE LA MARE

Music

When music sounds, gone is the earth I know,
And all her lovely things even lovelier grow;
Her flowers in vision flame, her forest trees
Lift burdened branches, stilled with ecstasies.

When music sounds, out of the water rise
Naiads whose beauty dims my waking eyes,
Rapt in strange dream burns each enchanted face,
With solemn echoing stirs their dwelling-place.

When music sounds, all that I was I am
Ere to this haunt of brooding dust I came;
While from Time's woods break into distant song
The swift-winged hours, as I hasten along.

WALTER DE LA MARE

Evening

When twilight darkens, and one by one,
The sweet birds to their nests have gone;
When to green banks the glow-worms bring
Pale lamps to brighten evening;
Then stirs in his thick sleep the owl,
Through the dewy air to prowl.

Hawking the meadow, swiftly he flits,
    While the small mouse a-trembling sits
With tiny eye of fear upcast
Until his brooding shape be past,
Hiding her where the moonbeams beat,
Casting black shadows in the wheat.

Now all is still: the field-man is
Lapped deep in slumbering silentness.
Not a leaf stirs, but clouds on high
Pass in dim flocks across the sky,
Puffed by a breeze too light to move
Aught but these wakeful sheep above.

O, what an arch of light now spans
These fields by night no longer Man's!
Their ancient Master is abroad,
Walking beneath the moonlight cold:
His presence is the stillness, He
Fills earth with wonder and mystery.

WALTER DE LA MARE

An Epitaph

Here lies a most beautiful lady,
Light of step and heart was she;
I think she was the most beautiful lady
That ever was in the West Country.

But beauty vanishes; beauty passes;
However rare—rare it be;
And when I crumble, who will remember
This lady of the West Country?

WALTER DE LA MARE

Fare Well

When I lie where shades of darkness
Shall no more assail mine eyes,
Nor the rain make lamentation
    When the wind sighs;
How will fare the world whose wonder
Was the very proof of me?
Memory fades, must the remembered
    Perishing be?

Oh, when this my dust surrenders
Hand, foot, lip, to dust again,
May those loved and loving faces
    Please other men!
May the rusting harvest hedgerow
Still the Traveller's Joy entwine,
And as happy children gather
    Posies once mine.

Look thy last on all things lovely,
Every hour.   Let no night
Seal thy sense in deathly slumber
    Till to delight
Thou have paid thy utmost blessing;
Since that all things thou wouldst praise
Beauty took from those who loved them
    In other days.

WALTER DE LA MARE

The Praise of Dust

'What of vile dust?' the preacher said.
    Methought the whole world woke,
The dead stone lived beneath my foot,
    And my whole body spoke.

'You, that play tyrant to the dust,
    And stamp its wrinkled face,
This patient star that flings you not
    Far into homeless space,

'Come down out of your dusty shrine
    The living dust to see,
The flowers that at your sermon's end
    Stand blazing silently.

'Rich white and blood-red blossom; stones,
    Lichens like fire encrust;
A gleam of blue, a glare of gold,
    The vision of the dust.

'Pass them all by: till, as you come
    Where, at a city's edge,
Under a tree—I know it well—
    Under a lattice ledge,

'The sunshine falls on one brown head.
    You, too, O cold of clay,
Eater of stones, may haply hear
    The trumpets of that day.

'When God to all His paladins
By His own splendour swore
To make a fairer face than heaven,
Of dust and nothing more.'

GILBERT KEITH CHESTERTON

After Apple-Picking

My long two-pointed ladder's sticking through a tree
Toward heaven still,
And there's a barrel that I didn't fill
Beside it, and there may be two or three
Apples I didn't pick upon some bough.
But I am done with apple-picking now.
Essence of winter sleep is on the night,
The scent of apples: I am drowsing off.
I cannot rub the strangeness from my sight
I got from looking through a pane of glass
I skimmed this morning from the drinking trough

And held against the world of hoary grass.
It melted, and I let it fall and break.
But I was well
Upon my way to sleep before it fell,
And I could tell
What form my dreaming was about to take.
Magnified apples appear and disappear,
Stem end and blossom end,
And every fleck of russet showing clear.
My instep arch not only keeps the ache,
It keeps the pressure of a ladder-round.
I feel the ladder sway as the boughs bend.
And I keep hearing from the cellar bin
The rumbling sound
Of load on load of apples coming in.
For I have had too much
Of apple-picking: I am overtired
Of the great harvest I myself desired.
There were ten thousand thousand fruit to touch,
Cherish in hand, lift down, and not let fall.
For all
That struck the earth,
No matter if not bruised or spiked with stubble,
Went sure to the cider-apple heap
As of no worth.
One can see what will trouble
This sleep of mine, whatever sleep it is.
Were he not gone,
The woodchuck could say whether it's like his
Long sleep, as I describe its coming on,
Or just some human sleep.

ROBERT FROST

The Tuft of Flowers

I went to turn the grass once after one
Who mowed it in the dew before the sun.

The dew was gone that made his blade so keen
Before I came to view the levelled scene.

I looked for him behind an isle of trees;
I listened for his whetstone on the breeze.

But he had gone his way, the grass all mown,
And I must be, as he had been,—alone,

'As all must be,' I said within my heart,
'Whether they work together or apart.'

But as I said it, swift there passed me by
On noiseless wing a bewildered butterfly,

Seeking with memories grown dim o'er night
Some resting flower of yesterday's delight.

And once I marked his flight go round and round
As where some flower lay withering on the ground.

And then he flew as far as eye could see,
And then on tremulous wing came back to me.

I thought of questions that have no reply,
And would have turned to toss the grass to dry;

But he turned first, and led my eye to look
At a tall tuft of flowers beside a brook.

A leaping tongue of bloom the scythe had spared
Beside a reedy brook the scythe had bared.

The mower in the dew had loved them thus,
By leaving them to flourish, not for us,

Nor yet to draw one thought of ours to him,
But from sheer morning gladness at the brim.

The butterfly and I had lit upon,
Nevertheless, a message from the dawn,

That made me hear the wakening birds around,
And hear his long scythe whispering to the ground,

And feel a spirit kindred to my own;
So that henceforth I worked no more alone;

But glad with him, I worked as with his aid,
And weary, sought at noon with him the shade;

And dreaming, as it were, held brotherly speech
With one whose thought I had not hoped to reach.

'Men work together,' I told him from the heart,
'Whether they work together or apart.'

ROBERT FROST

216

Stopping by Woods on a Snowy Evening

Whose woods these are I think I know.
His house is in the village though;
He will not see me stopping here
To watch his woods fill up with snow.

My little horse must think it queer
To stop without a farmhouse near
Between the woods and frozen lake
The darkest evening of the year.

He gives his harness bells a shake
To ask if there is some mistake.
The only other sound's the sweep
Of easy wind and downy flake.

The woods are lovely, dark and deep,
But I have promises to keep,
And miles to go before I sleep,
And miles to go before I sleep.

ROBERT FROST

The Wind and the Rain

Roman, Roman, what do you here?
Your great Wall is fallen this many a year—
Fallen, fallen, the Roman Wall;
And green grow the bent and the moss over all.

The wind and the rain have tumbled down
What the foemen left of tower and town.
Well and truly you builded your Wall,
But the wind and the rain are the masters of all:
Bravely you builded: but all in vain
Man builds against the wind and the rain:
The raking wind and the seeping rain,
Whatever man builds, unbuild again.
Man builds in vain, for the wind and the wet,
The water that saps and the airs that fret,
His pride of towers will overset.

Man builds: but all must fall as the Wall
You builded, O Roman, to breast the squall:
The wide-flung ramparts and cities tall
Must fall as the Wall—yea, all must fall,
And tempest ride over the ruins of all:
For the wind and the rain are the masters of all.

WILFRID WILSON GIBSON

Beauty

I have seen dawn and sunset on moors and windy hills
Coming in solemn beauty like slow old tunes of Spain:
I have seen the lady April bringing the daffodils,
Bringing the springing grass and the soft warm April rain.

I have heard the song of the blossoms and the old chant of
    the sea,
And seen strange lands from under the arched white sails of
    ships;
But the loveliest things of beauty God ever has showed to
    me,
Are her voice, and her hair, and eyes, and the dear red
    curve of her lips.

JOHN MASEFIELD

On Malvern Hill

A wind is brushing down the clover,
    It sweeps the tossing branches bare,
Blowing the poising kestrel over
    The crumbling ramparts of the Caer.

It whirls the scattered leaves before us
    Along the dusty road to home,
Once it awakened into chorus
    The heart-strings in the ranks of Rome.

16

There by the gusty coppice border
   The shrilling trumpets broke the halt,
The Roman line, the Roman order,
   Swayed forwards to the blind assault.

Spearman and charioteer and bowman
   Charged and were scattered into spray,
Savage and taciturn the Roman
   Hewed upwards in the Roman way.

There—in the twilight—where the cattle
   Are lowing home across the fields,
The beaten warriors left the battle
   Dead on the clansmen's wicker shields.

The leaves whirl in the wind's riot
   Beneath the Beacon's jutting spur,
Quiet are clan and chief, and quiet
   Centurion and signifer.

JOHN MASEFIELD

If I should ever by Chance

If I should ever by chance grow rich
I'll buy Codham, Cockridden, and Childerditch,
Roses, Pyrgo, and Lapwater,
And let them all to my elder daughter.
The rent I shall ask of her will be only
Each year's first violets, white and lonely,

The first primroses and orchises—
She must find them before I do, that is.
But if she finds a blossom on furze
Without rent they shall all for ever be hers,
Codham, Cockridden, and Childerditch,
Roses, Pyrgo, and Lapwater,—
I shall give them all to my elder daughter.

EDWARD THOMAS

Words

Out of us all
That make rhymes,
Will you choose
Sometimes—
As the winds use
A crack in a wall
Or a drain,
Their joy or their pain
To whistle through—
Choose me,
You English words?

I know you:
You are light as dreams,
Tough as oak,
Precious as gold,
As poppies and corn,
Or an old cloak:

Sweet as our birds
To the ear,
As the burnet rose
In the heat
Of Midsummer:
Strange as the races
Of dead and unborn:
Strange and sweet
Equally,
And familiar,
To the eye,
As the dearest faces
That a man knows,
And as lost homes are:
But though older far
Than oldest yew,—
As our hills are, old,—
Worn new
Again and again:
Young as our streams
After rain:
And as dear
As the earth which you prove
That we love.

Make me content
With some sweetness
From Wales
Whose nightingales
Have no wings,—
From Wiltshire and Kent
And Herefordshire,
And the villages there,—

From the names, and the things
No less.
Let me sometimes dance
With you,
Or climb
Or stand perchance
In ecstasy,
Fixed and free
In a rhyme,
As poets do.

EDWARD THOMAS

The Old Ships

I have seen old ships sail like swans asleep
Beyond the village which men still call Tyre,
With leaden age o'ercargoed, dipping deep
For Famagusta and the hidden sun
That rings black Cyprus with a lake of fire;
And all those ships were certainly so old
Who knows how oft with squat and noisy
   gun,
Questing brown slaves or Syrian oranges,
The pirate Genoese
Hell-raked them till they rolled
Blood, water, fruit and corpses up the hold.
But now through friendly seas they softly run,
Painted the mid-sea blue or shore-sea green,
Still patterned with the vine and grapes in
   gold.

223

But I have seen,
Pointing her shapely shadows from the dawn
And image tumbled on a rose-swept bay,
A drowsy ship of some yet older day;
And, wonder's breath indrawn,
Thought I—who knows—who knows—but in that same
(Fished up beyond Ææa, patched up new
—Stern painted brighter blue—)
That talkative, bald-headed seaman came
(Twelve patient comrades sweating at the oar)
From Troy's doom-crimson shore,
And with great lies about his wooden horse
Set the crew laughing, and forgot his course.

It was so old a ship—who knows, who knows?
—And yet so beautiful, I watched in vain
To see the mast burst open with a rose,
And the whole deck put on its leaves again.

JAMES ELROY FLECKER

Wiltshire Downs

The cuckoo's double note
Loosened like bubbles from a drowning throat
Floats through the air
In mockery of pipit, lark and stare.

The stable-boys thud by
Their horses slinging divots at the sky
And with bright hooves
Printing the sodden turf with lucky grooves.

As still as a windhover
A shepherd in his flapping coat leans over
His tall sheep-crook
And shearlings, tegs and yoes cons like a book.

And one tree-crowned long barrow
Stretched like a sow that has brought forth her farrow
Hides a king's bones
Lying like broken sticks among the stones.

ANDREW YOUNG

Teg = a yearling sheep.

Portrait of a Machine

What nudity as beautiful as this
Obedient monster purring at its toil;
These naked iron muscles dripping oil
And the sure-fingered rods that never miss.
This long and shining flank of metal is
Magic that greasy labour cannot spoil;
While this vast engine that could rend the soil
Conceals its fury with a gentle hiss.

It does not vent its loathing, it does not turn
Upon its makers with destroying hate.
It bears a deeper malice; lives to earn
Its master's bread and laughs to see this great
Lord of the earth, who rules but cannot learn,
Become the slave of what his slaves create.

LOUIS UNTERMEYER

The Eyes

Rest Master, for we be a-weary, weary
And would feel the fingers of the wind
Upon these lids that lie over us
Sodden and lead-heavy.

Rest brother, for lo! the dawn is without!
The yellow flame paleth
And the wax runs low.

Free us, for without be goodly colours,
Green of the wood-moss and flower colours,
And coolness beneath the trees.

Free us, for we perish
In this ever-flowing monotony
Of ugly print marks, black
Upon white parchment.

EZRA POUND

Free us, for there is one
Whose smile more availeth
Than all the age-old knowledge of thy books:
And we would look thereon.

EZRA POUND

Bat

At evening, sitting on this terrace,
When the sun from the west, beyond Pisa, beyond the
    mountains of Carrara
Departs, and the world is taken by surprise . . .
When the tired flower of Florence is in gloom beneath the
    glowing
Brown hills surrounding . . .
When under the arches of the Ponte Vecchio
A green light enters against stream, flush from the west,
Against the current of obscure Arno . . .
Look up, and you see things flying
Between the day and the night;
Swallows with spools of dark thread sewing the shadows
    together.
A circle swoop, and a quick parabola under the bridge
    arches
Where light pushes through;
A sudden turning upon itself of a thing in the air.
A dip to the water.
And you think:
'The swallows are flying so late!'
Swallows?

Dark air-life looping
Yet missing the pure loop . . .
A twitch, a twitter, an elastic shudder in flight
And serrated wings against the sky,
Like a glove, a black glove thrown up at the light,
And falling back.
Never swallows!
Bats!
The swallows are gone.
At a wavering instant the swallows give way to bats
By the Ponte Vecchio . . .
Changing guard.
Bats, and an uneasy creeping in one's scalp
As the bats swoop overhead!
Flying madly.
Pipistrello!
Black piper on an infinitesimal pipe.
Little lumps that fly in air and have voices indefinite, wildly
    vindictive;
Wings like bits of umbrella.
Bats!
Creatures that hang themselves up like an old rag, to sleep;
And disgustingly upside down.
Hanging upside down like rows of disgusting old rags
And grinning in their sleep.
Bats!
In China the bat is symbol of happiness.
Not for me!

DAVID HERBERT LAWRENCE

Piano

Softly, in the dusk, a woman is singing to me;
Taking me back down the vista of years, till I see
A child sitting under the piano, in the boom of the tingling
strings
And pressing the small, poised feet of a mother who smiles
as she sings.

In spite of myself, the insidious mastery of song
Betrays me back, till the heart of me weeps to belong
To the old Sunday evenings at home, with winter outside
And hymns in the cosy parlour, the tinkling piano our
guide.

So now it is vain for the singer to burst into clamour
With the great black piano appassionato. The glamour
Of childish days is upon me, my manhood is cast
Down in the flood of remembrance, I weep like a child for
the past.

DAVID HERBERT LAWRENCE

Everyone Sang

Everyone suddenly burst out singing;
And I was filled with such delight
As prisoned birds must find in freedom
Winging wildly across the white
Orchards and dark green fields; on; on; and out of sight.

Everyone's voice was suddenly lifted,
And beauty came like the setting sun.
My heart was shaken with tears, and horror
Drifted away. . . . O, but every one
Was a bird; and the song was wordless; the singing will
   never be done.

SIEGFRIED SASSOON

Clouds

Down the blue night the unending columns press
   In noiseless tumult, break and wave and flow,
   Now tread the far South, or lift rounds of snow
Up to the white moon's hidden loveliness.
Some pause in their grave wandering comradeless,
   And turn with profound gesture vague and slow,
   As who would pray good for the world, but know
Their benediction empty as they bless.

They say that the Dead die not, but remain
    Near to the rich heirs of their grief and mirth.
    I think they ride the calm mid-heaven, as these,
In wise majestic melancholy train,
    And watch the moon, and the still-raging seas,
And men, coming and going on the earth.

RUPERT BROOKE

Peace

Now, God be thanked Who has matched us with His hour,
    And caught our youth, and wakened us from sleeping,
With hand made sure, clear eye, and sharpened power,
    To turn, as swimmers into cleanness leaping,
Glad from a world grown old and cold and weary,
    Leave the sick hearts that honour could not move,
And half-men, and their dirty songs and dreary,
    And all the little emptiness of love!

Oh! we, who have known shame, we have found release
        there,
    Where there's no ill, no grief, but sleep has mending,
    Naught broken save this body, lost but breath;
Nothing to shake the laughing heart's long peace there
    But only agony, and that has ending;
    And the worst friend and enemy is but Death.

RUPERT BROOKE

The Soldier

If I should die, think only this of me:
    That there's some corner of a foreign field
That is for ever England. There shall be
    In that rich earth a richer dust concealed;
A dust whom England bore, shaped, made aware,
    Gave, once, her flowers to love, her ways to roam,
A body of England's, breathing English air,
    Washed by the rivers, blest by suns of home.
And think, this heart, all evil shed away,
    A pulse in the eternal mind, no less
        Gives somewhere back the thoughts by England given;
Her sights and sounds; dreams happy as her day;
    And laughter, learnt of friends; and gentleness,
        In hearts at peace, under an English heaven.

RUPERT BROOKE

Into Battle

The naked earth is warm with spring,
    And with green grass and bursting trees
Leans to the sun's gaze glorying,
    And quivers in the sunny breeze;
And Life is colour and warmth and light,
    And a striving evermore for these;
And he is dead who will not fight;
    And who dies fighting has increase.

The fighting man shall from the sun
  Take warmth, and life from the glowing earth;
Speed with the light-foot winds to run,
  And with the trees to newer birth;
And find, when fighting shall be done,
  Great rest, and fullness after dearth.

All the bright company of Heaven
  Hold him in their high comradeship,
The Dog-Star and the Sisters Seven,
  Orion's Belt and sworded hip.

The woodland trees that stand together,
  They stand to him each one a friend;
They gently speak in the windy weather;
  They guide to valley and ridge's end.

The kestrel hovering by day,
  And the little owls that call by night,
Bid him be swift and keen as they,
  As keen of ear, as swift of sight.

The blackbird sings to him, 'Brother, brother,
  If this be the last song you shall sing,
Sing well, for you may not sing another;
  Brother, sing.'

In dreary, doubtful, waiting hours,
  Before the brazen frenzy starts,
The horses show him nobler powers;
  O patient eyes, courageous hearts!

And when the burning moment breaks,
  And all things else are out of mind,
And only joy of battle takes
  Him by the throat, and makes him blind,

Through joy and blindness he shall know,
  Not caring much to know, that still
Nor lead nor steel shall reach him, so
  That it be not the Destin'd Will.

The thundering line of battle stands,
  And in the air Death moans and sings;
But Day shall clasp him with strong hands,
  And Night shall fold him in soft wings.

JULIAN GRENFELL

A Song for Simeon

Lord, the Roman hyacinths are blooming in bowls and
The winter sun creeps by the snow hills;
The stubborn season has made stand.
My life is light, waiting for the death wind,
Like a feather on the back of my hand.
Dust in sunlight and memory in corners
Wait for the wind that chills towards the dead land.

Grant us thy peace.
I have walked many years in this city,
Kept faith and fast, provided for the poor,
Hath given and taken honour and ease.

There went never any rejected from my door.
Who shall remember my house, where shall live my
   children's children
When the time of sorrow is come?
They will take to the goat's path, and the fox's home,
Fleeing from the foreign faces and the foreign swords.
Before the time of cords and scourges and lamentation
Grant us thy peace.
Before the stations of the mountain of desolation,
Before the certain hour of maternal sorrow,
Now at this birth season of decease,
Let the Infant, the still unspeaking and unspoken Word,
Grant Israel's consolation
To one who has eighty years and no to-morrow.

According to thy word.
They shall praise Thee and suffer in every generation
With glory and derision,
Light upon light, mounting the saints' stair.
Not for me the martyrdom, the ecstasy of thought and
   prayer,
Not for me the ultimate vision.
Grant me thy peace.
(And a sword shall pierce thy heart,
Thine also.)
I am tired with my own life and the lives of those after me,
I am dying in my own death and the deaths of those after
   me.
Let thy servant depart,
Having seen thy salvation.

THOMAS STEARNS ELIOT

The Hollow Men

Mistah Kurtz—he dead
A Penny for the old Guy

I

We are the hollow men
We are the stuffed men
Leaning together
Headpiece filled with straw.   Alas!
Our dried voices, when
We whisper together
Are quiet and meaningless
As wind in dry grass
Or rats' feet over broken glass
In our dry cellar.

Shape without form, shade without colour,
Paralysed force, gesture without motion;

Those who have crossed
With direct eyes to death's other kingdom
Remember us—if at all—not as lost
Violent souls, but only
As the hollow men
The stuffed men.

II

Eyes I dare not meet in dreams
In death's dream kingdom
These do not appear:
There, the eyes are

Sunlight on a broken column
There, is a tree swinging
And voices are
In the wind's singing
More distant and more solemn
Than a fading star.

Let me be no nearer
In death's dream kingdom
Let me also wear
Such deliberate disguises—
Rat's coat, crowskin, crossed staves
In a field
Behaving as the wind behaves
No nearer—

Not that final meeting
In the twilight kingdom.

III

This is the dead land
This is cactus land
Here the stone images
Are raised, here they receive
The supplication of a dead man's hand
Under the twinkle of a fading star.

Is it like this
In death's other kingdom?
Waking alone
At the hour when we are

Trembling with tenderness,
Lips that would kiss
Form prayers to broken stone.

IV

The eyes are not here
There are no eyes here
In this valley of dying stars,
In this hollow valley
This broken jaw of our lost kingdoms
In this last of meeting places
We grope together
And avoid speech
Gathered on this beach of the tumid river

Sightless, unless
The eyes reappear
As the perpetual star
And multifoliate rose
Of death's twilight kingdom
The hope only
Of empty men.

V

Here we go round the prickly pear
Prickly pear prickly pear
Here we go round the prickly pear
At five o'clock in the morning.

Between the idea
And the reality

THOMAS STEARNS ELIOT

Between the motion
And the act
Falls the Shadow

   For Thine is the Kingdom
Between the conception
And the creation
Between the emotion
And the response
Falls the Shadow

      Life is very long
Between the desire
And the spasm
Between the potency
And the existence
Between the essence
And the descent
Falls the Shadow

   For Thine is the Kingdom
For thine is
Life is
For Thine is the

This is the way the world ends
This is the way the world ends
This is the way the world ends
Not with a bang but a whimper.

THOMAS STEARNS ELIOT

THOMAS STEARNS ELIOT

Journey of the Magi

'A cold coming we had of it,
Just the worst time of the year
For a journey, and such a long journey:
The ways deep, and the weather sharp,
The very dead of winter.'
And the camels galled, sore-footed, refractory,
Lying down in the melting snow.
There were times we regretted
The summer palaces on slopes, the terraces,
And the silken girls bringing sherbet.
Then the camel men cursing and grumbling
And running away, and wanting their liquor and women,
And the night-fires going out, and the lack of shelters,
And the cities hostile and the towns unfriendly
And the villages dirty and charging high prices:
A hard time we had of it.
At the end we preferred to travel all night,
Sleeping in snatches,
With the voices singing in our ears, saying
That this was all folly.

Then at dawn we came down to a temperate valley,
Wet, below the snow-line, smelling of vegetation;
With a running stream and a water-mill beating the
  darkness,
And three trees on the low sky,
And an old white horse galloped away in the meadow.
Then we came to a tavern with vine-leaves over the lintel,
Six hands at an open door dicing for pieces of silver,
And feet kicking the empty wine-skins.

But there was no information, and so we continued
And arrived at evening, not a moment too soon
Finding the place; it was (you may say) satisfactory.

All this was a long time ago, I remember,
And I would do it again, but set down
This set down
This: were we led all that way for
Birth or Death? There was a Birth, certainly,
We had evidence and no doubt. I had seen birth and death,
But had thought they were different; this Birth was   ·
Hard and bitter agony for us, like Death, our death.
We returned to our places, these Kingdoms,
But no longer at ease here, in the old dispensation,
With an alien people clutching their gods.
I should be glad of another death.

THOMAS STEARNS ELIOT

Horses

Those lumbering horses in the steady plough,
On the bare field—I wonder why, just now,
They seemed terrible, so wild and strange,
Like magic power on the stony grange.

EDWIN MUIR

Perhaps some childish hour has come again,
When I watched fearful, through the blackening rain,
Their hooves like pistons in an ancient mill
Move up and down, yet seem as standing still.

Their conquering hooves which trod the stubble down
Were ritual that turned the field to brown,
And their great hulks were seraphim of gold,
Or mute ecstatic monsters on the mould.

And oh the rapture, when, one furrow done,
They marched broad-breasted to the sinking sun!
The light flowed off their bossy sides in flakes;
The furrows rolled behind like struggling snakes.

But when at dusk with steaming nostrils home
They came, they seemed gigantic in the gloam,
And warm and glowing with mysterious fire
That lit their smouldering bodies in the mire.

Their eyes as brilliant and as wide as night
Gleamed with a cruel apocalyptic light.
Their manes the leaping ire of the wind
Lifted with rage invisible and blind.

Ah, now it fades! it fades! and I must pine
Again for that dread country crystalline,
Where the blank field and the still-standing tree
Were bright and fearful presences to me.

EDWIN MUIR

242

The Combat

It was not meant for human eyes,
That combat on the shabby patch
Of clods and trampled turf that lies
Somewhere beneath the sodden skies
For eye of toad or adder to catch.

And having seen it I accuse
The crested animal in his pride,
Arrayed in all the royal hues
Which hide the claws he well can use
To tear the heart out of the side.

Body of leopard, eagle's head
And whetted beak, and lion's mane,
And frost-grey hedge of feathers spread
Behind—he seemed of all things bred.
I shall not see his like again.

As for his enemy, there came in
A soft round beast as brown as clay;
All rent and patched his wretched skin;
A battered bag he might have been,
Some old used thing to throw away.

Yet he awaited face to face
The furious beast and the swift attack.
Soon over and done.   That was no place
Or time for chivalry or for grace.
The fury had him on his back.

And two small paws like hands flew out
To right and left as the trees stood by.
One would have said beyond a doubt
This was the very end of the bout,
But that the creature would not die.

For ere the death-blow he was gone,
Writhed, whirled, huddled into his den,
Safe somehow there.   The fight was done,
And he had lost who had all but won.
But oh his deadly fury then.

A while the place lay blank, forlorn,
Drowsing as in relief from pain.
The cricket chirped, the grating thorn
Stirred, and a little sound was born.
The champions took their posts again.

And all began.   The stealthy paw
Slashed out and in.   Could nothing save
These rags and tatters from the claw?
Nothing.   And yet I never saw
A beast so helpless and so brave.

And now, while the trees stand watching, still
The unequal battle rages there,
And the killing beast that cannot kill
Swells and swells in his fury till
You'd almost think it was despair.

EDWIN MUIR

Making Cider

I saw within the wheelwright's shed
The big round cartwheels, blue and red;
A plough with blunted share;
A blue tin jug; a broken chair;
And paint in trial patchwork square
Slapped up against the wall;
The lumber of the wheelwright's trade,
And tools on benches neatly laid,
The brace, the adze, the awl;

And, framed within the latticed-panes,
Above the cluttered sill,
Saw rooks upon the stubble hill
Seeking forgotten grains;

And all the air was sweet and shrill
With juice of apples heaped in skips,
Fermenting, rotten, soft with bruise,
And all the yard was strewn with pips,
Discarded pulp, and wrung-out ooze
That ducks with rummaging flat bill
Searched through beside the cider-press
To gobble in their greediness.

The young men strained upon the crank
To wring the last reluctant inch.
They laughed together, fair and frank,
And threw their loins across the winch.

A holiday from field and dung,
From plough and harrow, scythe and spade,

To dabble in another trade,
To crush the pippins in the slats,
And see that in the little vats
An extra pint was wrung;
While round about the worthies stood,
Profuse in comment, praise or blame,
Content the press should be of wood,
Advising rum, decrying wheat,
And black strong sugar makes it sweet,
But still resolved, with maundering tongue,
That cider could not be the same
As once when they were young;
But still the young contemptuous men
Laughed kindly at their old conceit,
And strained upon the crank again.

Now barrels ranged in portly line
Mature through winter's sleep,
Aping the leisured sloth of wine
That dreams by Tiber or by Rhine,
Mellowing slow and deep;
But keen and cold the northern nights
Sharpen the quiet yard.
And sharp like no rich southern wine
The tang of cider bites;
For here the splintered stars and hard
Hold England in a frosty guard,
Orion and the Pleiades
Above the wheelwright's shed,
And Sirius resting on the trees
While all the village snores abed.

VICTORIA SACKVILLE-WEST

On the Coast of Coromandel

On the coast of Coromandel
Dance they to the tunes of Handel;
Chorally, that coral coast
Correlates the bone to ghost,
Till word and limb and note seem one,
Blending, binding act to tone.

All day long they point the sandal
On the coast of Coromandel.
Lemon-yellow legs all bare
Pirouette to peruqued air
From the first green shoots of morn,
Cool as northern hunting-horn,
Till the nightly tropic wind
With its rough-tongued, grating rind
Shatters the frail spires of spice.
Imaged in the lawns of rice
(Mirror-flat and mirror green
Is that lovely water's sheen)
Saraband and rigadoon
Dance they through the purring noon,
While the lacquered waves expand
Golden dragons on the sand—
Dragons that must steaming die
From the hot sun's agony—
When elephants, of royal blood,
Plod to bed through lilied mud,
Then evening, sweet as any mango,
Bids them do a gay fandango,
Minuet, jig or gavotte.

How they hate the turkey-trot,
The nautch-dance and the highland fling,
Just as they will never sing
Any music save by Handel
On the coast of Coromandel!

SIR OSBERT SITWELL

Strange Meeting

1918

It seemed that out of the battle I escaped
Down some profound dull tunnel, long since scooped
Through granites which titanic wars had groined.
Yet also there encumbered sleepers groaned,
Too fast in thought or death to be bestirred.
Then, as I probed them, one sprang up, and stared
With piteous recognition in fixed eyes,
Lifting distressful hands as if to bless.
And by his smile, I knew that sullen hall,
By his dead smile I knew we stood in Hell.
With a thousand fears that vision's face was grained;
Yet no blood reached there from the upper ground,

And no guns thumped, or down the flues made moan.
'Strange, friend,' I said, 'here is no cause to mourn.'
'None,' said the other, 'save the undone years,
The hopelessness. Whatever hope is yours,
Was my life also; I went hunting wild
After the wildest beauty in the world,
Which lies not calm in eyes, or braided hair,
But mocks the steady running of the hour,
And if it grieves, grieves richlier than here.
For by my glee might many men have laughed,
And of my weeping something had been left,
Which must die now. I mean the truth untold,
The pity of war, the pity war distilled.
Now men will go content with what we spoiled,
Or, discontent, boil bloody, and be spilled.
They will be swift with swiftness of the tigress,
None will break ranks, though nations trek from progress.
Courage was mine, and I had mystery,
Wisdom was mine, and I had mastery;
To miss the march of this retreating world
Into vain citadels that are not walled.
Then, when much blood had clogged their chariot-wheels,
I would go up and wash them from sweet wells,
Even with truths that be too deep for taint.
I would have poured my spirit without stint
But not through wounds; not on the cess of war.
Foreheads of men have bled where no wounds were.
I am the enemy you killed, my friend.
I knew you in this dark; for so you frowned
Yesterday through me as you jabbed and killed.
I parried; but my hands were loath and cold.
Let us sleep now. . . .'

WILFRED OWEN

1805

At Viscount Nelson's lavish funeral,
    While the mob milled and yelled about St Paul's,
A General chatted with an Admiral:

'One of your colleagues, Sir, remarked today
    That Nelson's *exit*, though to be lamented,
Falls not inopportunely, in its way.'

'He was a thorn in our flesh,' came the reply—
    'The most bird-witted, unaccountable,
Odd little runt that ever I did spy.

'One arm, one peeper, vain as Pretty Poll,
    A meddler, too, in foreign politics
And gave his heart in pawn to a plain moll.

'He would dare lecture us Sea Lords, and then
    Would treat his ratings as though men of honour
And play at leap-frog with his midshipmen!

'We tried to box him down, but up he popped,
    And when he'd banged Napoleon at the Nile
Became too much the hero to be dropped.

'You've heard that Copenhagen "blind eye" story?
    We'd tied him to Nurse Parker's apron-strings—
By G—d, he snipped them through and snatched the glory!'

'Yet,' cried the General, 'six-and-twenty sail
    Captured or sunk by him off Tráfalgár—
That writes a handsome *finis* to the tale.'

'Handsome enough.   The seas are England's now.
  That fellow's foibles need no longer plague us
He died most creditably, I'll allow.'

'And, Sir, the secret of his victories?'
  'By his unServicelike, familiar ways, Sir,
He made the whole Fleet love him, damn his eyes!'

ROBERT GRAVES

Almswomen

At Quincey's moat the squandering village ends,
And there in the almshouse dwell the dearest friends
Of all the village, two old dames that cling
As close as any true-loves in the spring.
Long, long ago they passed threescore-and-ten,
And in this doll's house lived together then;
All things they have in common, being so poor,
And their one fear, Death's shadow at the door.
Each sundown makes them mournful, each sunrise
Brings back the brightness in their failing eyes.
How happy go the rich fair-weather days
When on the roadside folk stare in amaze

At such a honeycomb of fruit and flowers
As mellows round their threshold; what long hours
They gloat upon their steepling hollyhocks,
Bee's balsams, feathery southernwood, and stocks,
Fiery dragons'-mouths, great mallow leaves
For salves, and lemon-plants in bushy sheaves,
Shagged Esau's-hands with fine green finger-tips.
Such old sweet names are ever on their lips.
As pleased as little children where these grow
In cobbled pattens and worn gowns they go,
Proud of their wisdom when on gooseberry shoots
They stuck eggshells to fright from coming fruits
The brisk-billed rascals; pausing still to see
Their neighbour owls saunter from tree to tree,
Or in the hushing half-light mouse the lane
Long-winged and lordly.
                                    But when those hours wane
Indoors they ponder, scared by the harsh storm
Whose pelting saracens on the window swarm,
And listen for the mail to clatter past
And church clock's deep bay withering on the blast;
They feed the fire that flings a freakish light
On pictured kings and queens grotesquely bright,
Platters and pitchers, faded calendars
And graceful hour-glass trim with lavenders.

Many a time they kiss and cry, and pray
That both be summoned in the selfsame day,
And wiseman linnet tinkling in his cage
End too with them the friendship of old age,
And all together leave their treasured room
Some bell-like evening when the may's in bloom.

                                    EDMUND BLUNDEN

Forefathers

Here they went with smock and crook,
   Toiled in the sun, lolled in the shade,
Here they mudded out the brook
   And here their hatchet cleared the glade:
Harvest-supper woke their wit,
Huntsman's moon their wooings lit.

From this church they led their brides,
   From this church themselves were led
Shoulder-high; on these waysides
   Sat to take their beer and bread.
Names are gone—what men they were
These their cottages declare.

Names are vanished, save the few
   In the old brown Bible scrawled;
These were men of pith and thew,
   Whom the city never called;
Scarce could read or hold a quill,
Built the barn, the forge, the mill.

On the green they watched their sons
   Playing till too dark to see,
As their fathers watched them once,
   As my father once watched me;
While the bat and beetle flew
On the warm air webbed with dew.

Unrecorded, unrenowned,
   Men from whom my ways begin,

Here I know you by your ground
  But I know you not within—
There is silence, there survives
Not a moment of their lives.

Like the bee that now is blown
  Honey-heavy on my hand,
From the toppling tansy-throne
  In the green tempestuous land—
I'm in clover now, nor know
Who made honey long ago.

EDMUND BLUNDEN

Stormcock in Elder

In my dark hermitage, aloof
From the world's sight and the world's sound,
By the small door where the old roof
Hangs but five feet above the ground,

I groped along the shelf for bread
But found celestial food instead:

For suddenly close at my ear,
Loud, loud and wild, with wintry glee,
The old unfailing chorister
Burst out in pride of poetry;
And through the broken roof I spied
Him by his singing glorified.

Scarcely an arm's-length from the eye,
Myself unseen, I saw him there;
The throbbing throat that made the cry,
The breast dewed from the misty air,
The polished bill that opened wide
And showed the pointed tongue inside:

The large eye, ringed with many a ray
Of minion feathers, finely laid,
The feet that grasped the elder-spray;
How strongly used, how subtly made
The scale, the sinew, and the claw,
Plain through the broken roof I saw;

The flight-feathers in tail and wing,
The shorter coverts, and the white
Merged into russet, marrying
The bright breast to the pinions bright,
Gold sequins, spots of chestnut, shower
Of silver, like a brindled flower.

Soldier of fortune, northwest Jack,
Old hard-times' braggart, there you blow

But tell me ere your bagpipes crack
How you can make so brave a show,
Full-fed in February, and dressed
Like a rich merchant at a feast.

One-half the world, or so they say,
Knows not how half the world may live;
So sing your song and go your way,
And still in February contrive
As bright as Gabriel to smile
On elder-spray by broken tile.

RUTH PITTER

The Serf

His naked skin clothed in the torrid mist
That puffs in smoke around the patient hooves,
The ploughman drives, a slow somnambulist,
And through the green his crimson furrow grooves.
His heart, more deeply than he wounds the plain,
Long by the rasping share of insult torn,
Red clod, to which the war-cry once was rain
And tribal spears the fatal sheaves of corn,
Lies fallow now.   But as the turf divides
I see in the slow progress of his strides
Over the toppled clods and falling flowers,
The timeless, surly patience of the serf
That moves the nearest to the naked earth
And ploughs down palaces, and thrones, and towers.

ROY CAMPBELL

The Zebras

From the dark woods that breathe of fallen showers,
Harnessed with level rays in golden reins,
The zebras draw the dawn across the plains
Wading knee-deep among the scarlet flowers.
The sunlight, zithering their flanks with fire,
Flashes between the shadows as they pass
Barred with electric tremors through the grass
Like wind along the gold strings of a lyre.

Into the flushed air snorting rosy plumes
That smoulder round their feet in drifting fumes,
With dove-like voices call the distant fillies,
While round the herds the stallion wheels his flight,
Engine of beauty volted with delight,
To roll his mare among the trampled lilies.

ROY CAMPBELL

The Caves

This is the cave of which I spoke,
These are the blackened stones, and these
Our footprints, seven lives ago.

Darkness was in the cave like shifting smoke,
Stalagmites grew like equatorial trees,
There was a pool, quite black and silent, seven lives ago

Here such a one turned back, and there
Another stumbled and his nerve gave out;
Men have escaped blindly, they know not how.

Our candles gutter in the mouldering air,
Here the rock fell, beyond a doubt,
There was no light in those days, and there is none now.

Water drips from the roof, and the caves narrow,
Galleries lead downward to the unknown dark;
This was the point we reached, the farthest known.

Here someone in the debris found an arrow,
Men have been here before, and left their mark
Scratched on the limestone wall with splintered bone.

Here the dark word was said for memory's sake,
And lost, here on the cold sand, to the puzzled brow.

This was the farthest point, the fabled lake:
These were our footprints, seven lives ago.

MICHAEL ROBERTS

The Conflict

I sang as one
Who on a tilting deck sings
To keep their courage up, though the wave hangs
That shall cut off their sun.

As storm-cocks sing,
Flinging their natural answer in the wind's teeth,
And care not if it is waste of breath
Or birth-carol of spring.

As ocean-flyer clings
To height, to the last drop of spirit driving on
While yet ahead is land to be won
And work for wings.

Singing I was at peace,
Above the clouds, outside the ring:
For sorrow finds a swift release in song
And pride its poise.

Yet living here,
As one between two massive powers I live
Whom neutrality cannot save
Nor occupation cheer.

None such shall be left alive:
The innocent wing is soon shot down,
And private stars fade in the blood-red dawn
Where two worlds strive.

The red advance of life
Contracts pride, calls out the common blood,
Beats song into a single blade,
Makes a depth-charge of grief.

Move then with new desires,
For where we used to build and love
Is no man's land, and only ghosts can live
Between two fires.

CECIL DAY LEWIS

The Ecstatic

Lark, skylark, spilling your rubbed and round
Pebbles of sound in air's still lake,
Whose widening circles fill the noon; yet none
Is known so small beside the sun:

Be strong your fervent soaring, your skyward air!
Tremble there, a nerve of song!
Float up there where voice and wing are one,
A singing star, a note of light!

Buoyed, embayed in heaven's noon-wide reaches—
For soon light's tide will turn—Oh stay!
Cease not till day streams to the west, then down
That estuary drop down to peace.

CECIL DAY LEWIS

Norfolk

How did the Devil come? When first attack?
　　These Norfolk lanes recall lost innocence,
The years fall off and find me walking back
　　Dragging a stick along the wooden fence
Down this same path, where, forty years ago,
My father strolled behind me, calm and slow.

I used to fill my hand with sorrel seeds
　　And shower him with them from the tops of stiles,
I used to butt my head into his tweeds
　　To make him hurry down those languorous miles
Of ash and alder-shaded lanes, till here
Our moorings and the masthead would appear.

There after supper lit by lantern light
　　Warm in the cabin I could lie secure
And hear against the polished sides at night
　　The lap lap lapping of the weedy Bure,
A whispering and watery Norfolk sound
Telling of all the moonlit reeds around.

How did the Devil come? When first attack?
  The church is just the same, though now I know
Fowler of Louth restored it. Time, bring back
  The rapturous ignorance of long ago,
The peace, before the dreadful daylight starts,
Of unkept promises and broken hearts.

JOHN BETJEMAN

Seaside Golf

How straight it flew, how long it flew,
  It clear'd the rutty track
And soaring, disappeared from view
  Beyond the bunker's back—
A glorious, sailing, bounding drive
That made me glad I was alive.

And down the fairway, far along
  It glowed a lonely white;
I played an iron sure and strong
  And clipp'd it out of sight,
And spite of grassy banks between
I knew I'd find it on the green.

And so I did. It lay content
  Two paces from the pin;
A steady putt and then it went
  Oh, most securely in.
The very turf rejoiced to see
That quite unprecedented three.

Ah! seaweed smells from sandy caves
  And thyme and mist in whiffs,
In-coming tide, Atlantic waves
  Slapping the sunny cliffs,
Lark song and sea sounds in the air
And splendour, splendour everywhere.

JOHN BETJEMAN

Fish in the Unruffled Lakes

Fish in the unruffled lakes
The swarming colours wear,
Swans in the winter air
A white perfection have,
And the great lion walks
Through his innocent grove;
Lion, fish, and swan
Act, and are gone
Upon Time's toppling wave.

We till shadowed days are done,
We must weep and sing
Duty's conscious wrong,
The Devil in the clock,
The Goodness carefully worn
For atonement or for luck;
We must lose our loves,
On each beast and bird that moves
Turn an envious look.

Sighs for folly said and done
Twist our narrow days;
But I must bless, I must praise
That you, my swan, who have
All gifts that to the swan
Impulsive Nature gave,
The majesty and pride,
Last night should add
Your voluntary love.

WYSTAN HUGH AUDEN

Look, Stranger

Look, stranger, at this island now
The leaping light for your delight discovers,
Stand stable here
And silent be,
That through the channels of the ear
May wander like a river
The swaying sound of the sea.

Here at the small field's ending pause
Where the chalk wall falls to the foam, and its tall ledges
Oppose the pluck
And knock of the tide,
And the shingle scrambles after the sucking surf, and the gull
    lodges
A moment on its sheer side.

Far off like floating seeds the ships
Diverge on urgent voluntary errands;
And the full view
Indeed may enter
And move in memory as now these clouds do,
That pass the harbour mirror
And all the summer through the water saunter.

WYSTAN HUGH AUDEN

A Dark World

Under the pent-house branches the eight swans have come,
Into the black-green water round the roots of the yew;
Like a beam descending the lake, the stairway to their room.

The young swans in their tender smoke-grey feathers, blown
By wind or light to a faint copper smouldering,
Come docile with their parents still, three-quarters grown.

The old swans, built of light like marble, tower and scatter
Light in the dusk; but the young are mate to the yew's shade.
With their dim-green webbed feet like hands they part the
    water

And wind among its loops and eyes of mercury,
Less visible than these they have wakened; and beside
The trellised roots they twine their necks as fine and grey.

In groups and in their fugue following one another
They turn to constant music their intercourse; and passing
With neck stretched on, with greyhound brow, brother by
    brother,

Or slowlier drawing level, where their mute and furled
Wings touch they loose a feather to float on the night-face
Of water, with white stars to drift as a dark world.

EDITH JOY SCOVELL

Evening

Pears from the boughs hung golden,
The street lay still and cool,
Children with books and satchels
Came sauntering home from school;
The dusk fled softly inward
Across each darkening sill,
The whole sweet autumn slumbered,
The street lay cool and still:

The children moved through twilight,
The village steeple gleamed,
Pears from their boughs hung trembling
And suddenly it seemed,
Shaken with such a wildness
Of terror and desire,
My heart burst into music
And my body into fire.

FREDERIC PROKOSCH

Seen in a Glass

Behind the tree, behind the house, behind the stars
Is the presence that I cannot see
Otherwise than as house and stars and tree.

Tree, house and stars
Extend to infinity within themselves
Into the mystery of the world

Where whirl the wheels of power whose pulses beat
Out of nothing, out of night,
Leaves, stones and fires,

The living tree whose maypole dance
Of chromosome and nucleus
Traces the maze of boughs and leaves,

The standing house of stone that poured
In molten torrent when was hurled
Out of chaos this great world,

And suns whose kindling begins anew
Or ends the course that tree, house, world move through,

Upheld by being that I cannot know
In other form than stars and stones and trees
Assume in nature's glass, in nature's eyes.

KATHLEEN RAINE

He will watch the Hawk

He will watch the hawk with an indifferent eye
  Or pitifully;
Nor on those eagles that so feared him, now
  Will strain his brow;
Weapons men use, stone, sling and strong-thewed bow
  He will not know.

This aristocrat, superb of all instinct,
    With death close linked
Had paced the enormous cloud, almost had won
    War on the sun;
Till now, like Icarus mid-ocean-drowned,
    Hands, wings, are found.

STEPHEN SPENDER

I think continually

I think continually of those who were truly great.
Who, from the womb, remembered the soul's history
Through corridors of light where the hours are suns,
Endless and singing. Whose lovely ambition
Was that their lips, still touched with fire,
Should tell of the Spirit, clothed from head to foot in song.
And who hoarded from the Spring branches
The desires falling across their bodies like blossoms.

What is precious, is never to forget
The essential delight of the blood drawn from ageless
 springs
Breaking through rocks in worlds before our earth.
Never to deny its pleasure in the morning simple light
Nor its grave evening demand for love.
Never to allow gradually the traffic to smother
With noise and fog, the flowering of the Spirit.

Near the snow, near the sun, in the highest fields,
See how these names are fêted by the waving grass
And by the streamers of white cloud
And whispers of wind in the listening sky.
The names of those who in their lives fought for life,
Who wore at their hearts the fire's centre.
Born of the sun, they travelled a short while toward the sun
And left the vivid air signed with their honour.

STEPHEN SPENDER

The Pylons

The secret of these hills was stone, and cottages
Of that stone made,
And crumbling roads
That turned on sudden hidden villages.

Now over these small hills they have built the concrete
That trails black wire:
Pylons, those pillars
Bare like nude, giant girls that have no secret.

The valley with its gilt and evening look
And the green chestnut
Of customary root,
Are mocked dry like the parched bed of a brook.

But far above and far as sight endures
Like whips of anger
With lightning's danger
There runs the quick perspective of the future.

This dwarfs our emerald country by its trek
So tall with prophecy:
Dreaming of cities
Where often clouds shall lean their swan-white neck.

STEPHEN SPENDER

For Dinah, the Adeneys' Cat

Thirty elongated seconds
By the sun
We stared, the cat and I,
Strangers, cool and crouched
Behind unwinking green

Till flick
Along the spine, a whip
Of recognition cut
Our masks of fur and skin,
Cat-o'-nine-tails with a sting
Neither hinted at
By curl of lip
Or spitting tongue.

Then one cat turned
With poise of air
And washed a spotless paw,
The other took a tortoiseshell comb
And almost yawned
As she combed her tatless hair.

ANNE WILKINSON

Fern House at Kew

Look! it is as though the sun,
Defrosting every spangled pane,
Should touch the fern engraven there
And turn it green again;
  Till the fronds, uncurling in
  The ice which held them captive, flow
  With water-music from the roof
  To tropic airs below;

And I, the boy who many a night
Fashioned in a jungle dream
The boat that I may never steer
Darkly against the stream,
   Quant the fathomed gangways, now,
   Brushed by all green things that grow.

Pondweed, here, without a pond
Wavers on the stagnant air,
Soft beside the trailing hand
Drifts the maidenhair
   And steeply to the lightless stream
   The tributary moonwort flows,
   Distilling on the river-bed
   A green light that glows.
Yet, by the cataract, how still
The prehistoric tendrils rise:
Antennae of enormous moth,
Spider with spores for eyes.
   Diluvian images, they stand
   Unstirring in an older land.

O yellow-hammered sun, my bird
In Paradise beyond the cage,
Sing to the fossil mind, unscale
The lizard eye of age;
   Till fireflies, juggling in the dark
   Above the duckboard ripples, turn
   Candescent as the speckled light
   That filters through the fern;
And humming birds in splendour thread
The tapestry a dreamer wove,

Slinging their scarlet shuttles through
The green warp of the grove.
  Now, behind the tall bamboo,
  Tiger lurks, and cockatoo.

The clock strikes one.   A shadow falls
On serpent-stripe and tortoiseshell.
The toucan lifts his melon beak
In token of farewell;
  For waterfowl are calling on
  The English ornamental pool,
  Where carrot-coloured goldfish swim
  And prams are put to cool.
Close the door.   Nor ever look
Behind you in the fronded pane.
Orpheus lost Eurydice,
And I must find again
  The little star-crossed boy at play
  A continent of years away.

PAUL DEHN

The Cranes

We thought they were gulls at first,
                    while they were distant—
The two cranes flying out of a normal morning.
They circled twice about our house and sank,
Their long legs drooping, down over the wood.
We saw their wings flash white, frayed at the black tip,
And heard their harsh cry, like a rusty screw.

Down in the next field, shy and angular,
They darted their long necks in the grass for fish.
They would not have us close, but shambled coyly,
Ridiculous, caught on the ground. Yet our fields
Under their feet became a fen; the sky
That was blue July became watery November,
And echoing with the cries of foreign birds.

ANNE RIDLER

The Giraffes

I think before they saw me the giraffes
Were watching me.   Over the golden grass,
The bush and ragged open tree of thorn,
From a grotesque height, under their lightish horns,
Their eyes were fixed on mine as I approached them.
The hills behind descended steeply: iron
Coloured outcroppings of rock half covered by
Dull green and sepia vegetation, dry
And sunlit: and above, the piercing blue
Where clouds like islands lay or like swans flew.

Seen from those hills the scrubby plain is like
A large-scale map whose features have a look
Half menacing, half familiar, and across
Its brightness arms of shadow ceaselessly
Revolve. Like small forked twigs or insects move
Giraffes, upon the great map where they live.

When I went nearer, their long bovine tails
Flicked loosely, and deliberately they turned,
An undulation of dappled grey and brown,
And stood in profile with those curious planes
Of neck and sloping haunches. Just as when
Quite motionless they watched I never thought
Them moved by fear, a desire to be a tree,
So as they put more ground between us I
Saw evidence that these were animals with
Perhaps no wish for intercourse, or no
Capacity.
                    Above the falling sun
Like visible winds the clouds are streaked and spun,
And cold and dark now bring the image of
Those creatures walking without pain or love.

ROY FULLER

The Lonely Farmer

Poor hill farmer astray in the grass;
There came a movement and he looked up, but
All that he saw was the wind pass.
There was a sound of voices on the air,

But where, where? It was only the glib stream talking
Softly to itself. And once when he was walking
Along a lane in spring he was deceived
By a shrill whistle coming through the leaves:
Wait a minute, wait a minute—four swift notes;
He turned, and it was nothing, only a thrush
In the thorn bushes easing its throat.
He swore at himself for paying heed,
The poor hill farmer, so often again
Stopping, staring, listening, in vain,
His ear betrayed by the heart's need.

R. S. THOMAS

The Kestrel

I watch a kestrel in the sky
Hover above the field and think
How to that concentrated eye
The teeming world entire must shrink
  Into a single mouse until
    He stoops to kill.

Yet from that corpse, cold as a stone,
The ripples ring, the abounding day
Goes circling outward, on and on,
Oblivious of the bird of prey—
  Time—that eventually will strike
    Down all alike.

PATRIC DICKINSON

The Swans

Midstream they met.   Challenger and champion,
They fought a war for honour
Fierce, sharp, but with no honour:
Each had a simple aim and sought it quickly.
The combat over, the victor sailed away
Broken, but placid as is the gift of swans,
Leaving his rival to his shame alone.
I listened for a song, according to story,
But this swan's death was out of character—
No giving up of the grace of life
In a sad lingering music.
I saw the beaten swan rise on the water
As though to outreach pain, its webbed feet
Banging the river helplessly, its wings
Loose in a last hysteria.   Then the neck
Was floating like a rope and the swan was dead.
It drifted away and all around it swan's-down
Bobbed on the river like children's little boats.

CLIFFORD DYMENT

For the Grieg Centenary

The fells are jagged in the shining air; the wind
Sharpens itself like a knife on the rough edges;
The sky is blue as ice, and clouds from the sea
    Splinter above the land
And drive against the rocks in thin steel wedges.

This of all England is the place to remember Grieg:
Here where the Norsemen foraged down the dales,
Crossing the sea with the migrant redwing,
    Thieving heifer and yow and teg,
Leaving their names scotched on the flanks of the hills.

Leaving also the crackling northern tongues,
The dialect crisp with the click of the wind
In the thorns of a wintry dyke,
    So that Solvieg sings
In the words which bind the homes of Cumberland.

Therefore let Solvieg sing in the western dales
When the frost is on the pikes, and the raven builds again
Its nest in February; let Crinkle Crags
    Be thumped by the humpbacked trolls,
And the voice of Grieg ring loud through the sound of the
    sea and the rain.

NORMAN NICHOLSON

And Death Shall Have No Dominion

And death shall have no dominion.
Dead men naked they shall be one
With the man in the wind and the west moon;
When their bones are picked clean and the clean bones gone,
They shall have stars at elbow and foot;
Though they go mad they shall be sane,
Though they sink through the sea they shall rise again;
Though lovers be lost love shall not;
And death shall have no dominion.

And death shall have no dominion.
Under the windings of the sea
They lying long shall not die windily;
Twisting on racks when sinews give way,
Strapped to a wheel, yet they shall not break;
Faith in their hands shall snap in two,
And the unicorn evils run them through;
Split all ends up they shan't crack;
And death shall have no dominion.

And death shall have no dominion.
No more may gulls cry at their ears
Or waves break loud on the seashores;
Where blew a flower may a flower no more
Lift its head to the blows of the rain;
Though they be mad and dead as nails,
Heads of the characters hammer through daisies;
Break in the sun till the sun breaks down,
And death shall have no dominion.

DYLAN THOMAS

Fern Hill

Now as I was young and easy under the apple boughs
About the lilting house and happy as the grass was green,
   The night above the dingle starry,
     Time let me hail and climb
    Golden in the heydays of his eyes,
And honoured among wagons I was prince of the apple
        towns
And once below a time I lordly had the trees and leaves
    Trail with daisies and barley
   Down the rivers of the windfall light.

And as I was green and carefree, famous among the barns
About the happy yard and singing as the farm was home,
   In the sun that is young once only,
     Time let me play and be
    Golden in the mercy of his means,
And green and golden I was huntsman and herdsman, the
      calves
Sang to my horn, the foxes on the hills barked clear and
      cold,
    And the sabbath rang slowly
   In the pebbles of the holy streams.

All the sun long it was running, it was lovely, the hay
Fields high as the house, the tunes from the chimneys, it was
     air
   And playing, lovely and watery
    And fire green as grass.
   And nightly under the simple stars
As I rode to sleep the owls were bearing the farm away,

All the moon long I heard, blessed among stables, the
    nightjars
  Flying with the ricks, and the horses
    Flashing into the dark.

And then to awake, and the farm, like a wanderer white
With the dew, come back, the cock on his shoulder: it was
    all
  Shining, it was Adam and maiden,
    The sky gathered again
  And the sun grew round that very day.
So it must have been after the birth of the simple light
In the first, spinning place, the spellbound horses walking
    warm
  Out of the whinnying green stable
    On to the fields of praise.

And honoured among foxes and pheasants by the gay house
Under the new made clouds and happy as the heart was
    long,
  In the sun born over and over,
    I ran my heedless ways,
  My wishes raced through the house high hay
And nothing I cared, at my sky blue trades, that time allows
In all his tuneful turning so few and such morning songs
  Before the children green and golden
    Follow him out of grace,

Nothing I cared, in the lamb white days, that time would
    take me
Up to the swallow thronged loft by the shadow of my hand,
  In the moon that is always rising,
    Nor that riding to sleep

I should hear him fly with the high fields
And wake to the farm forever fled from the childless land.
Oh as I was young and easy in the mercy of his means,
    Time held me green and dying
  Though I sang in my chains like the sea.

DYLAN THOMAS

King's College Chapel

When to the music of Byrd or Tallis,
The ruffed boys singing in the blackened stalls,
The candles lighting the small bones on their faces,
    The Tudors stiff in marble on the walls,

There comes to evensong Elizabeth or Henry,
    Rich with brocade, pearl, golden lilies, at the altar,
The scarlet lions leaping on their bosoms,
    Pale royal hands fingering the crackling psalter,

Henry is thinking of his lute and of backgammon,
  Elizabeth follows the waving song, the mystery,
Proud in her red wig and green jewelled favours;
  They sit in their white lawn sleeves, as cool as history.

CHARLES CAUSLEY

William Wordsworth

No room for mourning: he's gone out
Into the noisy glen, or stands between the stones
Of the gaunt ridge, or you'll hear his shout
Rolling among the screes, he being a boy again.
He'll never fail nor die
And if they laid his bones
In the wet vaults or iron sarcophagi
Of fame, he'd rise at the first summer rain
And stride across the hills to seek
His rest among the broken lands and clouds.
He was a stormy day, a granite peak
Spearing the sky; and look, about its base
Words flower like crocuses in the hanging woods,
Blank though the dalehead and the bony face.

SIDNEY KEYES

Greenwich Observatory

This onion-dome holds all intricacies
Of intellect and star-struck wisdom; so
Like Coleridge's head with multitudinous
Passages riddled, full of strange instruments
Unbalanced by a touch, this organism
From wires and dials spins introverted life.
It never looks, squat on its concrete shoulders,
Down at the river's swarming life, nor sees
Cranes' groping insect-like activity
Nor slow procession of funnels past the docks.
Turning its inner wheels, absorbed in problems
Of space and time, it never hears
Birds singing in the park or children's laughter.
Alive, but in another way, it broods
On this its Highgate, hypnotized
In lunar reverie and calculation.
Yet night awakes it; blind lids open
Leaden to look upon the moon:
A single goggling telescopic eye
Enfolds the spheric wonder of the sky.

SIDNEY KEYES

Giraffes

Beyond the brassy sun-stare where each shade
Crouches beneath its substance at mid-noon,
The tall giraffes are gathered in a glade
Grazing the green fruit of the midday moon.
Patched with sienna shadows of the jungle,
In pencil-slender attitudes they stand;
Grotesque in camouflage, each curve and angle
Is merged into the backcloth of the land.

These circus creatures of a poet's dreaming
Whose destiny on silent strings is spun,
Are patterned in design of nature's scheming
To move unseen through dappled woods and dun.
Strange genesis in which the substance seeming
The shadow, is the secret of the sun!

PHŒBE HESKETH

Nothing Grows Old

This is the hour the gods set to music:
Song in the branches, hope in the heart,
Rhythm in poplars like green spires adorning
The morning in tune with the moment apart.

Today is a soaring; and summit and steeple
And smoke from the clearing discover the sky.
Uncover the sky for us, upward-bound skylark—
The song will remain though the singer must die!

This is the peak of the measureless minute
That mankind aspires to and never can hold,
Disclosed in a flash by a primrose, a linnet—
The instant that tells us that nothing grows old!

PHŒBE HESKETH

Flight Into Egypt

They saw them pass, the old man limping, the donkey,
The hooded woman, riding sidesaddle,
And the bundle she held as if it were valuable.
They heard the beast sigh, for sand scattering
Rose under wind as vision under an eyelid.
And the four went veiled
Into the dark which swallowed them up in Egypt.

Who had seen this could understand
Neither the woman's diligence, nor the reason
For the false dawns flickering behind them ;
How in the old man's face all Egypt lay reflected ;
Nor could they see, through the enfolding cloth,
How wide looked up the pearl eyes of the flying god.

CHRISTOPHER MIDDLETON

INDEX OF FIRST LINES

INDEX OF AUTHORS